The Bass Angler's Almanac

Books Previously Published by John Weiss

1976   ADVANCED BASS FISHING, E.P. Dutton

1977   ADVANCED BASS FISHING, Stoeger Sportsman's Library

1978   HUNTING GEAR YOU CAN MAKE, The Outdoor Life Book Club

1979   THE WHITETAIL DEER HUNTER'S HANDBOOK, Winchester Press

1981   TRAIL COOKING, The Outdoor Life Book Club

1982   TRAIL COOKING, VanNostrand Reinhold

1982   CARE & COOKING OF FISH & GAME, Winchester Press

1983   OUTDOOR COOKERY, The Outdoor Life Book Club

1984   VENISON!, The Outdoor Life Book Club

1985   ADVANCED BASS FISHING, The Outdoor Life Book Club

1987   ADVANCED DEER HUNTING, The Outdoor Life Book Club

1993   THE PANFISHERMAN'S BIBLE, Doubleday

1993   THE ADVANCED DEER HUNTER'S BIBLE, Doubleday

1995   THE OUTDOOR CHEF'S BIBLE, Doubleday

2000   THE WHITETAIL DEER HUNTER'S ALMANAC, The Lyons Press

The Bass Angler's Almanac

More Than 650 Tips and Tactics

John Weiss

The Lyons Press
Guilford, Connecticut
An imprint of The Globe Pequot Press

Dedication

For my father, Bill, who introduced me to bass fishing at age 6. This was 50 years ago, back when anglers used steel casting rods, crude levelwind reels that had horrendous reputations for backlashing, and black braided-nylon lines. The favorite lures of the time were the Heddon Bass-o-Reno and the Johnson Silver Minnow, its hook draped with a strip of white porkrind. Oh yes, we also used rental wooden boats that leaked like sieves, and we rowed to our fishing hotspots. One tactic that Dad believed to be critically important for angling success was to always speak in soft whispers or, better yet, not talk at all, so as not to spook any fish that might be near our boat. How times have changed.

The Lyons Press is an imprint of The Globe Pequot Press.

Printed in United States of America

Designed by Compset, Inc.

10 9 8 7 6

Library of Congress Cataloging-in-Publication Data

Weiss, John, 1994–
 The bass angler's almanac/John Weiss.
  p. cm.
 ISBN 978-1-58574-471-8
 1. Bass fishing. I. Title.

SH681 .W414 2001
799.1'773—dc21   2001029217

CONTENTS

Introduction

The rapid rate at which our knowledge of bass behavior has increased in recent years makes compiling a comprehensive book on bass fishing a formidable challenge.

Bass have inhabited North American waters for tens of thousands of years, and yet 95 percent of what we know about the species—their habits in various types of water, methods of catching them consistently under a variety of conditions, and even effective management techniques—has been learned during only the past three decades. Moreover, our knowledge is increasing so rapidly that it's incredibly difficult for any fishing writer to keep abreast of the almost-monthly press releases describing new findings by the nation's biologists. Even more taxing, press releases from tackle and marine companies describing the latest rods, reels, lures, lines, and boating equipment arrive in our mailboxes on an almost daily basis!

So where does a fishing writer begin? Indeed, is it even possible for anyone to correlate the enormous and continually growing amount of angling know-how with the relevant, but oftentimes obscure, biological facts to produce a book that is not only readable but comprehensive? Probably not. It's unlikely that any single person will ever know everything there is to know about bass behavior and successful bass fishing. To add to a writer's confusion, not to mention his reader's bewilderment, even the most highly respected fisheries biologists often disagree on various facets of bass behavior.

Despite these difficulties, it's necessary to periodically assemble bass-fishing information from diverse sources into a single book that is as up to date as possible. However, unlike other previously published bass fishing books, this one takes a different approach. You won't find much here in the way of flowery prose or adventuresome anecdotes. Nor will you find an over-zealous emphasis upon product hype, because I firmly believe one cannot buy bass-fishing success; with basic, serviceable equipment, bass-fishing success is essentially free for the learning. What you will find instead are hundreds of quick-read, factual tips and insights I've gleaned from the country's most proficient guides, tournament pros, tackle manufacturers, and fishing scientists. These people, with whom I've had the privilege of sharing thousands of fishing hours, are not armchair anglers; nor are they self-ordained know-it-alls. They're still students themselves, who never spend a day on the water without learning something new. And they're teachers who are dedicated to helping average anglers with average means become much better fishermen.

That being said, look upon this almanac as a quick reference to be consulted often. When you run headlong into a problem during a frustratingly tough day on the water and you feel defeated, look on the positive side: You've learned something—what **doesn't** work. Then, take a few minutes to thumb through the appropriate section of this book that deals with the specific circumstances you encountered, and you'll learn what **will** work next time you're confronted with similar conditions.

John Weiss
Chesterhill, Ohio
May 2001

1

40 Insights About Largemouth Bass Biology

An essential component of bass-fishing success is knowing how the quarry, geared by its physiology, operates within its environment.

North Americans aren't the only anglers who enjoy fishing for largemouths. The fish have been transplanted to many other countries around the globe.

1. Biologists have identified 11 strains and/or species of bass. Some, such as the redeye bass, Suwanee bass, and Guadalupe bass, are found only in very restricted habitat niches such as certain rivers. The two most widespread and sought-after species are the largemouth bass (*Micropterus salmoides*) and the Florida

bass (*Micropterus salmoides floridanus*), which is a subspecies of the largemouth that has been stocked in waters stretching across the deep South, from Florida to California.

2. Alaska is the only state that does not have at least one strain of bass. Canada possesses the largemouth, smallmouth, and spotted bass, but not the Florida strain. Japan has the largemouth. Mexico, Honduras, and Cuba have the Florida strain of largemouth. South America and Africa have the largemouth. Many small countries, too numerous to mention but nearly all in latitudes south of the equator, possess largemouths.

3. The largemouth is primarily an inhabitant of natural lakes, man-made reservoirs, sluggish rivers, tide zones, farm ponds, strip-mine pits, and quarries. It's also an occasional resident of swift rivers and streams, but the fish doesn't thrive in cooler, rushing waters—in most such rivers and streams the species almost never reaches its maximum growth potential. In such environments it almost exclusively resides in quiet, deep pools out of the main current or along shorelines where heavy cover or bank configurations retard the current velocity.

4. Although the largemouth and its Florida cousin are commonly referred to as "black bass," this term is gradually falling out of usage, partly because the two fish are not always black in color. Since their coloration is a biological means of adapting to their environments, they may vary in color from region to region and even within the same body of water. In thick, vegetative areas, the fish are most commonly a vibrant grass-green color along the sides, darker toward the dorsal area, with a dirty-white underbelly. When the fish live in tannin-stained or brackish water, however, their coloration may be so dark that they do indeed appear black in color. In clear, open-water areas where there is a sandy or rocky bottom, the fish take on a tan color. And in milky or muddy water, the fish may appear pale green or even silvery. The sides of largemouths have splotchy markings that become pronounced in dark-colored or heavily vegetative water, and are believed to aid the fish in concealment while lying in ambush.

5. A thin, dark lateral line located midway along the sides of the largemouth, running from the gill flaps to the tail, is used in conjunction with a hidden inner ear to detect vibrations and other sounds in the water. This lateral line is more pronounced in fingerling bass, allowing them to more easily blend in with

The Florida bass, a subspecies of the largemouth, is our largest, but its range is restricted to warm, southern waters stretching from Florida to California.

Largemouths have the ability to change their coloration so as to blend with the particular water color, vegetation, or bottom conditions they are in at a given time.

the thin grassfields of the shallow water where they live the first two years of their lives.

6. An angler can easily distinguish a largemouth or its Florida sub-species from a smallmouth or spotted bass. When the mouth of a largemouth is closed, the rear of the upper jaw extends back past a vertical, imaginary line drawn from the rear edge of the eye. The forward portion of the spiny dorsal fin and the rear soft portion are nearly separated from one another, whereas in the other bass species the dorsal fins are either continuous or more nearly so.

7. It's usually very difficult for anglers to distinguish a largemouth bass from a Florida-strain largemouth. Biologists differentiate between the two by counting the number of rows of scales between the lateral line and the forward-most part of the dorsal fin. The largemouth has seven rows of scales and the Florida bass from seven to nine.

8. Although they commonly seem to have the ability to outsmart anglers, largemouths actually have very small brains and are incapable of high-level thinking. Moreover, as captives of their watery environment, they have no control over it; all they can

do is adapt to the periodic changes of their world. Nature assists this process by giving bass keen survival instincts, capable senses, fast reflexes, and an innate sense of caution.

9. The relatively short, truncated body shape of the largemouth indicates that this particular fish species is equipped to maneuver in and around tight cover and ambush prey at close range with short bursts of speed. Its body shape is not designed for swimming at sustained speeds in open-water pursuit of prey.

10. Aside from the largemouth's stocky shape, its chief distinguishing physical characteristic is its enormous mouth, which enables it to swallow large and varied prey. It feeds primarily upon baitfish, panfish, the young of other gamefish species, crayfish, aquatic insects, and amphibians such as frogs and salamanders. However, stomach-analysis studies of largemouths have revealed the fish clearly are opportunists, and will feed on snakes, birds, newborn waterfowl, rodents (such as mice), and fresh- and brackish-water shrimp.

11. Many fish species, including northern pike and muskellunge, are almost exclusively sight feeders, and are rarely caught after dark. Other fish species such as catfish feed primarily by smell, which means they rarely strike at artificial lures. But largemouths are generalist feeders. With sharp vision, keen hearing, and a highly developed sense of smell, they can feed under the widest range of underwater conditions, making them excellent candidates for the angler using either live baits or artificial lures.

12. Largemouths are classified as a cold-blooded species, which means their body temperature is always close to the temperature of the water surrounding them.

13. Largemouths also are classified as a warmwater species, which means they are most active when the temperature is 60°F or higher. This is in contrast to cold-water species such as salmon, char, and some trout species, which thrive best at temperatures below 60°F and in fact cannot even survive at temperatures that are much higher.

14. When the water temperature is warm (above 50°F) a largemouth's digestion of food requires an average of 18 hours. When the water temperature is cool or cold (below 50°F) it can take 30 hours to digest its last meal, and when the water temperature is lower than 40°F it can take 48 to 50 hours to digest its most recent food intake.

Although largemouths may strike at virtually any lure color, biologists have determined that strike frequency is highest with red and white or solid yellow colors.

15. New York biologists F.A. Brown and George Bennett, in laboratory studies, determined that largemouths can see a wide range of colors and, on occasion, may strike at any lure color they perceive as being food. They also determined that the strike frequency was highest with lures that were red and white or solid yellow in color.

16. Despite their superior predatory skills, largemouths go through lengthy periods of relative dormancy during which they feed little, if at all. These spells of reduced feeding are usually brought on by changes in water or weather conditions (such as cold

fronts or wintery cold-water periods) or by changes in the fish's biological condition (such as occur during spawning).

17. During winter in the northern states, largemouths technically do not go into hibernation. But the very cold water makes them lethargic, causing them to have a food intake of less than one-tenth of what they might have in summer. This causes no physiological harm to the fish because their body metabolism becomes so retarded that they expend a minimum amount of energy.

18. Largemouths are very efficient feeders, and have the instinctive ability to determine the food value of a potential prey item in terms of the energy that must be expended to catch it.

19. Many anglers have long believed that dawn and dusk are the best times to entice bass into striking at lures or taking live baits. Biologists say, however, that largemouths have no preferential feeding times. Moreover, they explain that the reason average anglers commonly catch more bass at dawn and dusk is because, in the low light levels of these time periods, bass are less likely to detect the clumsiness of their lure and bait presentations. This seems to be confirmed by bass fishing tournaments, in which the pros typically bring in huge catches of bass but are restricted to fishing during the hours of 8:00 a.m. to 3:00 p.m.

20. Given a food choice consisting of another fish species, largemouths distinctly prefer elongated, soft-ray species such as those found in the minnow family rather than high-profile, spiny-ray species such as bluegills, simply because they're easier to swallow. Keep this in mind when considering lure selection.

21. During warmwater months when largemouths are exhibiting peak activity levels, a given fish must consume a daily amount of food equal to one percent of its body weight in order to maintain its body weight. To continue growing, however, it must consume forage equaling two to three percent of its body weight each day.

22. Ice fishermen occasionally catch largemouths while angling for cool-water species such as walleyes, northern pike, or yellow perch. However, because the bass' body metabolism is so retarded at this time, they're rarely caught on jigging spoons or other artificial lures; rather, winter bass are normally taken on live bait fished in a stationary manner.

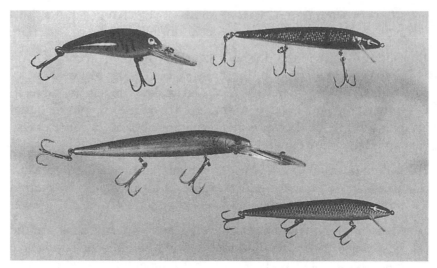

Bass forage heavily upon preyfish, but given a choice they prefer elongated, soft-ray species that are easier to swallow than stocky, spiny-ray species. Keep this in mind when choosing lures.

23. The largemouth possesses a swim bladder in its abdominal cavity, just below its spinal column. The swim bladder is an airtight pouch that the fish can slightly inflate or deflate to overcome gravity and suspend itself at arbitrary depths without effort. This is quite often done when bass are hovering for prolonged periods over spawning nests. It's also done when they are relating to a specific depth level where there is a desirable water temperature, pH band, oxygen-content level, or even when positioning themselves below a surface-swimming school of baitfish. Neutral-buoyancy lures are specifically geared to bass that are suspending, because once the lure is cranked down to a given depth level, and the retrieve is slowed, it remains at that specific depth.

24. Largemouths possess nostrils, but they play no role in breathing; utilizing dissolved oxygen in the water is strictly the role of the gill rakers located beneath the gill flaps. Rather, the nostrils, in conjunction with taste buds on the tongue and upper lip, are used to continually smell and taste the water as the fish searches for food. The nostrils and taste buds also monitor the water chemistry for unfavorable levels of salinity, alkalinity, or pollution, so that, once identified, those areas can be avoided.

25. Unlike many other gamefish species, a largemouth's fins are lo-cated much farther forward on the body's anatomy. This allows the fish to easily maneuver in any direction, including putting its transmission in reverse gear, to slowly and adroitly feed in the crevices and other bottom-cover irregularities where forage such as crayfish may be hiding. The largemouth's broad tail and strong musculature toward the rear of its body anatomy allows for brief speed bursts to catch prey attempting to flee.

26. Many anglers like to use very light tackle to enjoy the bass' pro-longed fighting attributes. Yet savvy anglers disagree with this, contending that tackle must be stout enough to quickly land a fish that is destined to be released. Their attitude is based upon scientist's findings that when largemouths are forced to overex-ert themselves for lengthy periods, their bodies experience a high level of oxygen depletion, causing body waste residues (primar-ily lactic acid) to build up in their musculature and greatly reduce their chances of survival upon release.

Many anglers prefer tackle that's heavy enough to land bass quickly, to ensure their survival upon release. A prolonged fight with light tackle causes lactic acid build-up that often causes a released bass to perish.

27. In large, specially equipped aquariums, largemouths in hot pursuit of prey have been clocked at 12 miles per hour for short bursts. Although this obviously suits the bass' needs, it is slow compared to salmon and striped bass, which can achieve 20 miles per hour. Compare that to sailfish and swordfish, which can achieve 60-mile-per-hour bursts of speed.

28. When largemouths forage, they do not consume food items by engulfing them in their mouths or biting down upon them. Instead, the instant they are within close range of the intended prey item, they open their mouth widely while simultaneously flaring their gill covers. This creates a strong suction effect not unlike that of a vacuum cleaner, allowing them to literally inhale the food item, sometimes from as much as 12 inches away.

29. The largemouth has two types of "ears." One is the lateral line along the exterior sides of the body, which is used to detect strong, low-frequency sounds that may come from any direction. The other is an inner ear that detects subtle high-frequency sounds passing through the water. This inner ear can only detect sounds coming from the direction in which the fish is facing, whereupon they are transmitted through the bass' skull to the inner ear.

30. Recall this book's dedication to my father, who always insisted upon talking very quietly to avoid spooking nearby fish. We now know that almost 100 percent of the sounds carried in the air are deflected by the water's surface and therefore do not affect bass at all.

31. Underwater, sounds travel much farther and faster than through air; tests by the U.S. Navy have determined that underwater sounds travel approximately 5,000 feet per second. Largemouths readily detect these sounds, particularly if an airborne sound is transmitted to the water through a solid object. Talk as much as you like, but be careful not to accidentally bang a paddle against the hull of a canoe or allow the lid of your boat's rod locker to slam shut.

32. Largemouths are adept at distinguishing the normal vibrations emitted by healthy, swimming baitfish as compared to the distress vibrations emitted by injured prey. This is why anglers fishing with minnows commonly cut part of the tail away to make the offering more attractive. It's also why plugs with built-in

rattles are so popular, as are lures that gurgle and sputter such as spinnerbaits, buzzbaits, and topwater plugs with propeller blades fore and aft.

33. Anatomically, the eyes of largemouths are remarkably similar to those of human beings. They contain rods, for the detection of movement and to aid in feeding in low-light levels. They also possess cones for discerning a wide range of colors. One thing largemouth eyes lack, on the other hand, are protective eyelids, making them very light-sensitive. Since bass cannot "squint" in bright light, their tendency is to lurk in the shadows afforded by cover or to retreat into deep water where sunlight penetration is retarded.

34. In contrast to human eyes, a largemouth's eyes are round, not flat, and this causes them to be nearsighted. This is not a disadvantage because a lack of clarity in most bodies of water limits long-range visibility anyway. The fish compensate for this by using their senses of smell, taste, and hearing to detect the nearby presence of prey species, and then bringing their eyes into use at the last minute as they make a short speed-burst to capture the food item.

35. Being round in shape, each of a bass' eyes has a visual arc of almost 180 degrees in all directions, to the top, to the bottom, and to both sides. Due to the progressively narrowing shape of the head, their forward vision overlaps slightly to also give them a binocular-like perspective of what's nearby. There is just a narrow, several-degree blind spot immediately to the rear.

36. While bass are always on the lookout for prey, they're also on full alert for predators larger than they are. On northern lakes, where toothy northern pike and muskies often patrol the open waters, bass cling tightly to shallow cover. Yet in southern waters, where bass are usually at the top of the food chain, they freely wander open areas far from the safety of cover.

37. North of the Mason-Dixon line, a trophy largemouth is usually considered to be a fish of five pounds or more. But in the deep South, where anglers may encounter the Florida strain of bass, you'll need to net one better than 10 pounds. In southern California, where the Florida strain of largemouth gorges upon a heavy diet of nutritious rainbow trout, bragging rights go to those who land fish in excess of 15 pounds.

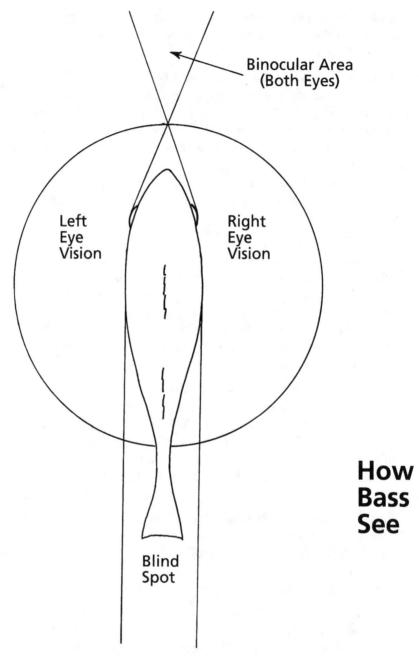

Binocular Area
(Both Eyes)

Left
Eye
Vision

Right
Eye
Vision

**How
Bass
See**

Blind
Spot

*Bass have a 340-degree field of view. Due to the shape and
placement of their eyes, the only thing that escapes their notice is
within a 20-degree blind spot immediately behind them.*

The biggest largemouths are always females. This 21-pounder, taken in southern California, is the second largest ever recorded.

38. In any region of the country, or any body of water, it's always the females of each bass species that attain the greatest weights. Males rarely grow larger than three or four pounds. Affectionate labels such as "sows," "hawgs," "bucketmouths," "mules," and "horses" are always in reference to female bass.

39. None of the bass species live year-round in any one place in any body of water. They are not a truly migratory species like walleyes or salmon. But within their home ranges they do make

seasonal movements (generally less than a quarter-mile) and shorter, temporary movements (sometimes only 20 yards) on a daily or even hourly basis.

40. As largemouths grow older and larger, they have a tendency to become more restricted in their movements. Compared to young bass that often engage in chase-and-catch feeding behavior, sometimes roaming in schools, larger bass are more sedentary, preferring to wait in solitary ambush for their prey.

2

34 Insights About Smallmouth and Spotted Bass Biology

Some refer to "brownies" and "spots" as those "other" bass, but they're challenging adversaries in their own right.

Smallmouth bass were originally native only to northern river systems but have since been transplanted to countless lakes and reservoirs.

1. Many anglers may be surprised to learn that largemouth, small-mouth, and spotted bass are not true bass. Rather, they're members of the sunfish family and therefore more closely related to bluegills than to true bass such as striped, white, and yellow bass.

2. The smallmouth bass (*Micropterus dolomieui*) originally was native only to northern river systems and natural Canadian shield lakes. Thanks to transplanting efforts, the species now inhabits a range almost identical to that of the largemouth. Since it favors slightly cooler water temperatures, it's found a bit farther north than the largemouth and, by the same token, is not plentiful in the desert Southwest. It is rarely found outside the contiguous United States and Canada.

Spotted bass were originally native only to southern river systems, where they seldom grew larger than two pounds. Now, inhabiting countless man-made reservoirs, they grow much larger. This Alabama nine-pounder, a former world record, was recently was eclipsed by a 10-pounder.

3. The spotted bass (*Micropterus punctulatus*) is sometimes also known as the Kentucky bass, although the species is not restricted to the state of Kentucky. Like the smallmouth, it also favors slightly cooler water temperatures than the largemouth; unlike the smallmouth, it predominantly inhabits waters across the South and Midwest. The spotted bass was originally native only to river systems, but the species has long since been transplanted into man-made reservoirs. It is rarely found in countries other than the United States, and its "spotty" occurrence elsewhere is due strictly to transplanting.

4. The physical anatomy and sensory apparatus of the smallmouth and spotted bass are almost identical to the largemouth's, and they operate in almost identical fashion. It's not necessary to repeat what was said in Chapter 1, so only significant differences will be noted.

5. Although the smallmouth is nicknamed "the brown bass," it's not universally brown in color but, like the largemouth, adapts to the

environment in which it lives. Generally, in rivers and streams, and in infertile northern lakes where the habitat is mostly sand and rock, the species takes on a bronze hue on the upper two-thirds of the body, with a yellowish-brown underbelly. In fertile, heavily vegetated lakes, however, the smallmouth's coloration is a more greenish-bronze. The smallmouth's lateral line is not as distinct as that of the largemouth—but, like the largemouth, the smallmouth has an average of three dark stripes fanning out from the snout to the rear of the gill covers, yielding to darker, irregular splotches along the sides of the body.

6. In waters inhabited by both largemouths and smallmouths, one way to tell the difference between the two is that the rear of the upper jaw does not extend beyond the eye when the mouth of the smallmouth is closed. Also, the forward and rear (spiny and rayed) portions of the dorsal fin are joined.

7. The spotted bass shares coloration characteristics of both the largemouth and smallmouth, depending upon its environment. In clear, weedy lakes it may take on a pale-green coloration, yet in off-colored river systems it may appear silvery. The spotted bass has the pronounced lateral line of the largemouth, yet its mouth is like that of a smallmouth in that the rear corner of the upper jaw extends to, but not beyond, the eye. Unique to this species, however, are irregular splotches on the upper (dorsal) half of the body and several rows of dark dots along the lower (ventral) region extending full length from the gill flaps to the base of the tail.

8. The mouths of smallmouth and spotted bass are comparable in size in relation to their bodies, and both are smaller than the largemouth's maw.

9. As mentioned in Chapter 1, biologists confirm a bass species identification by counting the rows of scales between the lateral line and the front of the dorsal fin. The spotted bass has nine rows of scales and the smallmouth has 11.

10. Another unique anatomical feature of the spotted bass, one not possessed by either the largemouth or smallmouth, has to do with its tongue. Open the fish's mouth and run your finger over the tongue and you'll feel a small, oval patch of very soft teeth; the tongues of largemouth, Florida-strain, and smallmouth bass are smooth to the touch.

Spotted bass are easily distinguished from largemouths and smallmouths by the rows of dots along the ventral region and an oval-shaped patch of soft teeth on the tongue.

11. Neither the spotted bass nor the smallmouth grows as large as the largemouth. The current world-record largemouth bass is just a bit more than 22 pounds. The current world-record smallmouth bass is just a bit more than 12 pounds, with a five- or six-pounder being a trophy. The world-record spotted bass is just a bit more than ten pounds, with a three- or four-pound "spot" considered a lunker.

12. Indiana biologist Elgin Ciampi, in laboratory studies, determined that largemouths have the most acute color vision of all freshwater fish species. The second and third species most adept at discerning colors are smallmouths and spotted bass, respectively, followed by muskies, northern pike, rainbow trout, crappies, and bluegills.

13. Like largemouths, smallmouths and spotted bass are cold-blooded creatures, meaning their body temperature is always nearly identical to that of the water surrounding them. But unlike largemouths, smallmouths and spotted bass are classified as cool-water, warm-water species. This means they are most active in those environments where the water temperature seldom if ever exceeds 70°F.

14. Since the most active body metabolism of smallmouths and spotted bass is in cooler water temperatures than that of largemouths, their food-digestion process occurs at a faster rate even when they inhabit a region of a lake where largemouths are also present.

15. Illinois biologist W. M. Lewis, who conducted studies on both northern and southern lakes and rivers, determined that crayfish account for 60 percent of a smallmouth's diet. In southern bodies of water, the remaining 40 percent of the fish's diet consists of open-water baitfish such as threadfin or gizzard shad or herring. In northern waters, however, the presence of northern pike, muskies, and walleyes prevents smallmouths from patrolling mid-lake regions, forcing them to remain in relatively shallow water, where they forage on small perch, leeches, shiners, various minnow species, hellgrammites (the larva of the Dobson fly), and other insects and amphibians.

16. Smallmouths are rarely found at depths greater than 30 feet, simply because this is the deepest level at which their primary forage—crayfish—lives.

Smallmouths and spotted bass forage heavily upon crayfish, except in those waters also inhabited by northern pike, muskies, and walleyes.

17. Many bottom conditions that may be tolerated by other bass species won't do for smallmouths. They're quite averse, for example, to soft-bottom conditions comprised of mud, muck, mire, loose soil, and silt. They're likewise averse to hard-bottom conditions over which there is abundant vegetation such as heavily matted weeds. Because of this, the common angler-held belief that the smallmouth is a hardy and tenacious species is really very far from the truth—at least if we use the largemouth's ready adaptability to myriad habitat conditions as a benchmark.

18. An ideal smallmouth lake or reservoir is usually rather expansive, with depths of at least 25 feet. Moreover, such waters possess only modest fertility levels (that is, the bottom composition is low in nitrogen compounds and other nutrients), causing plantlife to be relatively sparse. The bottom and its many associated structures is generally composed of sand, gravel, fractured sedimentary rock, hard-packed clay, marl (a mixture of clay and limestone), shale, or any combination of these materials.

19. Since the most productive smallmouth lakes and reservoirs are those with low fertility, the water tends to be exceptionally clear. Of course, variations occur—often during temporary upsets in

weather conditions—but the water usually ranges from crystal clear to slightly green or blue.

20. For any flowing waterway to sustain a healthy smallmouth population, it must have a gradient of no less than 4 feet per mile and no more than 20 feet per mile. Intermittent, shallow riffles with bottoms composed of sand, gravel, small rocks and boulders should separate long glides containing occasional deep pools.

21. Missouri biologists Phillip Smith and Lawrence Page determined that the forage intake of an average adult spotted bass can be broken down as follows: 39 percent crayfish, 33 percent small baitfish, 28 percent insects.

22. Both smallmouths and spotted bass engage in far more chase-and-catch feeding behavior than largemouths. To increase their efficiency, nature has given each species unique ducts inside their gill flaps that excrete a slime that passes back over their bodies as they swim, thus reducing friction and turbulence. This allows them to achieve their maximum swimming speed without having to expend all their energy.

Plugs and jigs that resemble crayfish are top lures for smallmouths and spotted bass. Otherwise, stick with lures that resemble small baitfish.

Smallmouths and spotted bass commonly inhabit the slow-moving water below hydroelectric dams.

23. Smallmouths and spotted bass both have hearing apparatuses that are structurally similar to that of the largemouth's, but not nearly as refined. Unlike the largemouth, which generally resides in quiet-water environments and must be able to detect the most subtle, low-key sounds of forage moving about, smallmouths and spotted bass don't require such sensitive hearing. Their environment commonly includes turbulent or at least slow-moving water, as in rivers or man-made reservoirs created for flood control or hydroelectric power generation. As a result, the moving water masks most underwater sounds, requiring the predators to rely almost exclusively upon sight in order to feed. True, spotted bass and smallmouths do inhabit quiet lake waters, but only as transplants; they evolved as river fish.

24. One favorable trait possessed by smallmouths is their ability to survive in water having low oxygen-saturation levels. Largemouths and spotted bass require at least 5 parts per million (ppm) of dissolved oxygen, but prefer 9 to 12 ppm, whereas smallmouths can make do with only 3 ppm.

25. Smallmouths are not nearly as tolerant of excessive water turbidity or variations in water temperature as the other bass species are. Any minor degradation of the smallmouth's habitat, such as an insignificant rise in pollution levels or acid rain contamination,

When several days of hot weather in early spring causes ice-out and warms the shallows, smallmouths and spotted bass can be caught almost immediately. Largemouths may not bite until weeks later, however.

which largemouths and spotted bass may be able to take in stride, usually leads to drastic reductions of smallmouth populations.

26. Although spotted bass inhabit many lakes, reservoirs, and rivers across the Midwest, and are quite active at colder water temperatures than largemouths prefer, they do not do well in bodies of water that freeze over for prolonged periods during winter. Biologists believe the reduced oxygen levels in iced-over lakes may play a role in this occurrence.

27. It's common for bodies of water that contain spotted bass to also contain largemouths and smallmouths. One noted exception that puzzles biologists is Allatoona Lake in northwestern Georgia, where more than 90 percent of all bass caught are spots, even though the lake has periodically been stocked with largemouths and smallmouths.

28. Although spotted bass are common in many river systems, they do much better in terms of reproduction and growth rates in

large highland reservoirs, found south of the Tennessee Valley, which are at least 25 feet deep. Further, the shoreline of one of these highland reservoirs typically includes high rock bluffs, ledges, shale slides, and outcroppings that drop off steeply at the water's edge. The bottom is usually rather hard, consisting of gravel, rocks, sand, clay, crumbled shale, hard-packed soil, or any combination of these materials.

29. Other features of ideal spotted bass lakes and reservoirs include standing or felled timber and brush on the bottom, with under-water structure consisting of points, bars, ridges, humps, and winding riverbeds and stream channels. There will also be feeder tributaries gushing into the body of water; while these are some-times short, narrow, and rather steep cuts along the shoreline, they are usually long creek arms.

30. In lakes and reservoirs, spotted bass are tied very closely to crayfish when they are using bank features in less than 25 feet of water. But frequently they pack up in schools to roam mid-lake areas at suspended levels to feed upon surface-swimming schools of gizzard or threadfin shad.

31. Spotted bass have been known to go much deeper than large-mouths and smallmouths—sometimes to 100 feet or more. That is really of little concern for the prospecting spotted bass angler, who will have great difficulty working deeper than 45 or 50 feet anyway.

32. Unlike with largemouths and smallmouths, midday produces much better catches of spotted bass. But as with largemouths and smallmouths, full dark can also be a time of spotted bass activity.

33. In rivers and streams, spotted bass can tolerate cooler and swifter water than largemouths, but they do not prefer the low water temperatures and current favored by smallmouths. So if you find a location that doesn't seem just right for either large-mouths or smallmouths, it may be perfect for spots.

34. Although spotted bass prefer different types of rivers and streams to those of largemouths and smallmouths, they like the same structure and bottom composition as their cousins. Look for them over clean, hard-bottom materials wherever you find brush, logs, or sweepers (shoreline trees that have fallen, with their crowns now underwater). Spotted bass are not often caught in weeds, unless other, preferred types of cover are not available.

CHAPTER

3

30 Tips for Reading
Maps and Using Sonar

*Maps and depthsounders serve as eyes that
allow us to see below the surface to find where
bass are living.*

When fishing a huge man-made reservoir or other large body of water, anglers who use maps and sonar can quickly home in on bass that may be widely scattered and in different stages of activity.

1. Never underestimate the value of maps in helping to find your way around on an unfamiliar body of water. Many man-made reservoirs are more than 50 miles in length and are characterized by countless interconnecting river systems, mile-long creek arms, and embayments so large you can barely see the shoreline on the other side.

2. Topographical maps (called topo maps for short), put out by the U.S. Geological Survey (USGS), are extremely popular with bass anglers. To get maps for waters in your region, contact the USGS, Map Distribution Center, 1200 South Eads St., Arlington, VA 22202, for areas east of the Mississippi. For areas west of the Mississippi, contact the USGS, Federal Center, Denver, CO 80225. Either office will first send a (free) quadrangle reference sheet and an order form for you to request maps of specific areas. The maps cost about $6 apiece. Topo maps for your immediate home area also are commonly available at local bookstores and engineering offices.

3. On some topo maps, man-made reservoirs may not appear as bodies of water; you'll simply see contour lines where the reservoir presently is. In this case, check with the local managing agency of the reservoir and ask for the "pool level" number; this is the elevation of the surface of the water under normal conditions. Then, using a felt-tipped marking pen, darken that numbered contour line on your map and you'll eventually have an outline of the entire body of water. You can also ask the managing agency of the reservoir if they have on file contour topo maps of the reservoir.

4. Second in popularity are hydrological charts. These are compiled by agencies such as the U.S. Army Corps of Engineers and Tennessee Valley Authority, which are charged with managing bodies of water for flood control or hydroelectric power generation. Such maps are usually available from each agency branch office at each body of water. Each lakeside office can also place your orders for hydro charts of agency-managed waters located elsewhere. They're about the same price as topo maps.

5. Topo maps and hydro charts are seldom as up to date as most anglers would like because they are reverified only once every 18 to 20 years. In the meantime, many changes can take place. Shoreline erosion, land slippage, or the entire falling away of a rock facing may alter shallow bottom contours. On bodies of water subjected to significant wind and wave action, underwater mid-lake features such as sandbars, shoals, reefs, and submerged islands may be partly obliterated and new ones created. If an area has been dredged to facilitate boat traffic, new underwater ridges, channels, and edges may have been created. If a bass angler sees such changes with his sonar, he should update his map with a felt-tipped pen.

6. An easy way to avoid some of the drawbacks and inconveniences of standard topo and hydro charts is to use specialized fishing charts now being compiled by private map companies. These companies take topo and hydro maps of the largest and most popular lakes and reservoirs nationwide and reverify their underwater terrain features about once every five years. These maps cost from $10 to $25 apiece. Check the classified ads of popular fishing magazines for the names and addresses of such companies. Such maps are also commonly available at tackle and bait shops that are typically located near each body of water.

Topo maps and hydrological charts are invaluable to serious bass anglers. So are specialized fishing maps that show more cover features and lakeside facilities.

7. Another advantage of so-called fishing maps produced by private companies is that they're usually published in atlas format and on specially treated paper that is impervious to weather and water. Unlike topo maps and hydro charts, they won't become reduced to a mushy glob if they become wet. Simply shake the map off and continue fishing.

8. Still another advantage of fishing maps compiled by private companies is that they're made specifically for fishermen. This means that, in addition to showing bottom contours, depths, and so on, they provide much more information of interest to anglers. Surrounding the lake proper, you'll see the locations of access roads, marinas, launch ramps, campgrounds, docks, piers, and so on. Also indicated are the underwater locations of stump fields, sandbars, clambeds, perennial weedbeds, canefields, submerged brush, standing timber, and countless other forms of cover and structure. In many cases, such maps also note general areas where various fish species are most frequently caught; this can be a great shortcut if you're on a weeklong fishing outing and want to devote a day or two to something other than bass, such as walleyes or stripers.

9. Always spend some time studying your map before going fishing. In particular, become familiar with the map legend. This is a small block somewhere on the face of the map that indicates how bottom structures and other features are represented on that particular chart.

10. Although there are exceptions, on most maps the dry terrain surrounding the body of water is usually shown in yellow or light brown. Very shallow water is usually shown in white, moderate depths are indicated in light blue, intermediate depths in light green, and the deepest water in dark blue. Inundated stream channels and riverbeds winding along the floor of the lake are shown as solid blue or black dotted lines. Old roads are indicated as parallel dashes. Drowned railroad spurs are represented by single lines with perpendicular cross-marks. Swamps are presented with symbols that look like rising suns. Submerged or standing timber, stumps, and brush may be indicated by single black dots or "puffball" marks. Vegetation is indicated by green, horizontal dashes.

11. Among the most important features on topo maps, hydro charts, and fishing maps are the contour lines that indicate both depth and how rapidly or slowly the bottom depth changes at a particular location. Lines that are very close together indicate a very rapid change in depth. In some places, contour lines may be so close together as to appear to form a single, heavy black line, which represents an abrupt drop-off. Conversely, the farther apart contour lines are spaced, the more gradual the underwater slope.

12. Contour lines that are close together and clearly run a long distance are frequently referred to as "breaklines." The majority of natural lakes and man-made reservoirs have at least two breaklines, but sometimes several more that stairstep their way down into the main lake basin. It's unusual for a body of water to have a smooth, bowl-like shape with no well-defined breaklines.

13. Seldom are the breaklines around a lake or reservoir equidistant or parallel to each other. Usually, as a reflection of the higher shoreline terrain, breaklines may in places meander in close to the shore or wander far away from it toward midlake areas, and in so doing will take on the appearances of long bars, points, and other structures.

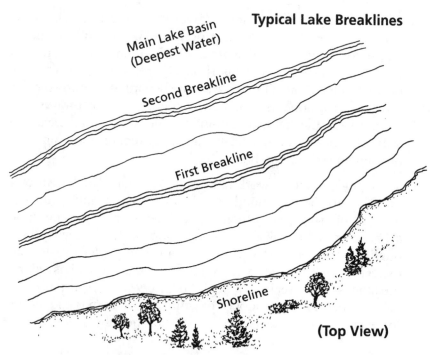

Typical Lake Breaklines

Main Lake Basin
(Deepest Water)

Second Breakline

First Breakline

Shoreline

(Top View)

The most notable features of any lake or reservoir are the two or more breaklines that completely encircle every body of water. (Top view)

**Typical Lake Breaklines
(Side View)**

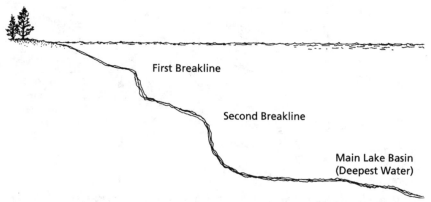

First Breakline

Second Breakline

Main Lake Basin
(Deepest Water)

Breaklines are drop-offs that stairstep into the depths of the main lake basin. (Side view)

14. Bass of all species commonly travel back and forth along the lengths of breaklines searching for food. They just as commonly pause for various lengths of time at certain places where a breakline is interrupted. This is usually referred to as a "break on a breakline." Such breaks are usually natural features such as rockpiles, stumpfields, clambeds, indentations, or protrusions. On occasion they're also man-made features such as discarded slabs of concrete, artificial fish shelters or reefs made from tires, or even an old sunken boat.

15. Many anglers like to work rather quickly along the length of a breakline for perhaps hundreds of yards, using assorted lures or live-bait offerings. They then pause whenever they come upon a break on a breakline, not continuing on until they've thoroughly worked it. The reason is because an angler usually can expect to pick up only widely scattered, individual bass along breaklines. At a break on a breakline, however, it's just as common to encounter a school of bass. It can sometimes take hours (or even days) to find such a school, but then the action is usu-

Typical Breaks on Breaklines

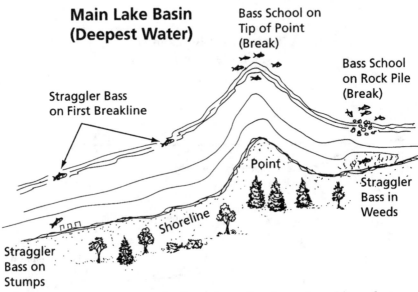

Main Lake Basin (Deepest Water)

Bass School on Tip of Point (Break)

Bass School on Rock Pile (Break)

Straggler Bass on First Breakline

Point

Straggler Bass in Weeds

Shoreline

Straggler Bass on Stumps

All three bass species may be found randomly on breaklines but they have a tendency to congregate at breaks, or structural interruptions on the breaklines.

ally fast and furious, with many good fish boated in a brief period of time from a relatively small spot.

16. Conversely, other anglers prefer almost exclusively to work much shallower than a lake's first two breaklines. As with the breakline angler, they catch only "straggler" bass but derive more enjoyment from having shoreline targets such as stumps, logs, and weedlines to cast to.

17. Sonar is one of the greatest advances in fishing in the past 50 years. There are many brands and types, ranging from portable units powered by dry-cell batteries to semipermanent gimbal units that run off a boat's 12-volt battery.

18. The three most common types of sonar are: the simple flasher unit, in which a whirring neon dial indicates the bottom depth and intermediate "spikes" reveal mid-depth features such as stumps or even fish; the graph recorder, which actually produces a paper printout of the bottom as the boat passes over it, showing the depth, shape of the bottom contour beneath the boat, and "crescents" representing fish; and the LCD (liquid crystal display), which shows the same things as the graph recorder but has a memory-recall feature instead of a paper printout.

The value of various types of sonar units is that, in addition to revealing the water depth and the shape of the bottom beneath the boat, they also indicate the presence of fish.

19. Sonar prices range from as low as $100 to as high as $2000. However, a high-quality unit for bass fishing purposes should not exceed $400, since it's not necessary to pay for special features that a bass angler rarely if ever needs. Features such as an integrated GPS (global positioning system) or a depth-capability reading to 500 feet are intended for anglers fishing for other species on the most expansive bodies of water.

20. Sonar features that are indeed important to the bass angler are a minimum of 125 screen pixels for the sharpest picture, total waterproof construction, vibration-proof mounting hardware, a circuit breaker for electrical surge protection, and advanced signal processing (which constantly evaluates and corrects for varying conditions such as boat speed). Also, make sure the unit under consideration has a sharp "grayline" feature. This is a band of gray color that helps to separate fish and important structure on or very near the bottom.

21. Portable depthsounders, in the form of flasher units or small LCD units, are ideal for the small-boat angler working small lakes, municipal city reservoirs, and large farm ponds.

22. Most serious bass anglers fishing larger lakes and reservoirs from bassboats or deep V-hull boats rely upon as many as two or three sonar devices. Typically, there may be a dashboard flasher unit the angler can monitor when quickly searching large areas at moderate speeds; when he finds something interesting, and shuts down the outboard and moves to the bow-mounted electric motor, he then uses a forward-deck-mounted LCD unit to take a closer look. Still other anglers who do not have a dash-mounted flasher use a gimbal-mounted graph recorder or LCD on the dash console and a second LCD on the bow platform. Personal preference is what generally dictates who uses what models.

23. The main disadvantage of a flasher unit is that everything from the surface to the bottom is displayed in the form of continuously flashing spikes of light, which not only must be interpreted correctly but are sometimes seen for only fractions of a second. Consequently, you must keep your eyes glued to the dial to be sure you don't miss something. On the other hand, graph recorders and LCD units create a permanent record of what the sonar sees; the angler doesn't have to continuously watch the screen and can even go back at a later time to more carefully study his sonar results.

The most common use of a console-mounted sonar device involves motoring over areas that you suspect hold bass, and checking for their presence.

24. The heart of a sonar device is a probe called the transducer, which transmits a "cone" of sound waves into the water. These impulses bounce off the bottom, return to the transducer, and are then translated into meaningful data that appears on the sonar screen. The water depth at that location is recorded, but so are the degree of hardness (or softness) of the bottom and the shape of the bottom contour. Anything that is in between

the surface and the bottom (fish, boulders, stumps, standing timber) is likewise recorded. Some sonar models also record the water temperature at various depths.

25. Nowadays, the transducer is epoxied inside the hull on most fiberglass bassboats. Installed during construction, this eliminates having an exterior-hull apparatus that creates water drag and is exposed and vulnerable to damage. The transducer impulses travel right through the hull with no loss of energy. Coupling the transducer to the sonar unit of choice is quick and easy; the angler merely inserts the sonar's connection wire into a universal transducer jack.

26. On most new, factory-rigged aluminum V-bottom boats, the transducer is mounted against the inside of the hull, usually in a livewell, with sheet-metal screws. In some cases, the transducer, in a mounting bracket, is attached to the exterior, bottom edge of the transom, as far to one side or the other as possible so outboard-prop cavitation doesn't disrupt the sonar signals.

27. Whether it's a fiberglass bassboat or an aluminum V-bottom, the sonar mounted on the dash console is always coupled to a transducer located near the stern. This allows the angler to continually read the bottom depth and obtain other information while the boat is under way.

28. If something interesting is discovered, such as fish or a likely bottom structure, the angler can then shut down the outboard and move to the bow seat. From there he can test-fish the area while monitoring his bow-mounted sonar and maneuvering with his electric motor. It's important to note that this bow-mounted sonar should not be coupled to the same stern-mounted transducer that the console-mounted sonar is plugged into, even though you can do this with two-way jacks if you want to. Otherwise, if the boat is 18 to 22 feet long, and the angler is up front, the data appearing on the bow-mounted sonar screen is from an area 18 to 22 feet behind where he's presently working his lures!

29. Make sure the bow-mounted sonar transducer is attached to the electric motor's shaft with a mounting bracket made specifically for that purpose. In this manner, the information appearing on the sonar screen is what exists directly beneath where the angler is sitting or standing.

In addition to a console-mounted sonar device, many anglers like to also have a bow-mounted sonar so that, once bass are located, they can efficiently fish the structure they've found.

30. No matter which style of sonar device an angler may find to his liking, he should always study the owner's manual. It contains a wealth of information and should be kept onboard in a plastic bag so it can be referred to on a moment's notice.

4

42 Facts About Bass Spawning Behavior

Bass are highly predictable in spring, but you'll still need a few tricks up your sleeve to be successful at catching them.

1. There is nothing disruptive to bass spawning behavior by catching them when they are in one of their three spawning stages. Although most anglers prefer to carefully release them, upon which the fish will quickly return to their previous location and activity, biologists say there is nothing harmful to a large lake's overall bass population by occasionally keeping a few fish for the table.

2. Any discussion of the various bass species must always bear qualifications such as "generally," "usually," and "most often." This is especially the case with regard to their spawning behavior. Prolonged spells of cold weather may delay spawning in some regions, while unseasonably hot weather may trigger early egg laying elsewhere. Radical fluctuations in water level due to heavy rains, drought, or flood control manipulation of a reservoir may, during some years, cause bass to nest much deeper than usual; other years, nests already constructed may suddenly find themselves high and dry, causing the absence of an entire age group of young bass.

3. There are three spawning stages. First is the *prespawn* stage, in which bass move to their spawning grounds in large numbers and are quite responsive to lures and live baits. Next comes the *spawning* stage, in which the fish are actually on their created nests and engaged in laying and fertilizing eggs; during this period the fish do not actively feed, but strike responses can be elicited. Finally comes the *postspawn* stage, in which the spent females drift away from the nests and go into a brief, almost comatose recuperative period. Male largemouths remain at the nesting site to protect the newly hatched fry; they recover from spawning and resume feeding almost immediately.

4. While water depth determines where the fish will spawn, water temperature determines *when* they will spawn. Largemouths engage in the most purposeful spawning when the water temperature reaches 65°F.

5. Smallmouth bass prefer slightly cooler water for spawning. Their most purposeful spawning gets underway as soon as the water temperature reaches 60°F.

6. Spotted bass begin actively spawning as soon as the water temperature reaches 62° to 65°F. In a lake that contains all three bass species, spotted bass generally begin moving onto their beds just after the smallmouths and just before the largemouths.

Where Lake Areas Warm First in Spring

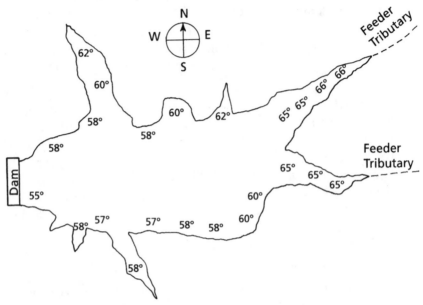

Largemouths, smallmouths, and spotted bass have different pre-ferred spawning temperatures. By monitoring various lake areas with a water temperature gauge, an angler can learn which stage of spawning a given species is in.

7. With regard to all three bass species, if the water repeatedly reaches their ideal spawning temperature, but then falls 5°F or more, the bass leave their beds and move back into holding stations in deeper water. Many times, repeated delays or "false spawns" ruin the reproduction cycle for that year because the roe-laden females eventually refuse to go back onto the beds; after a period of time, their bodies actually begin to absorb the eggs.

8. If, at a given lake, you regularly catch one- and two-pound bass, and four- and five-pound bass, but never any three-pounders, chances are that that particular age class was eliminated for one reason or another.

9. Latitude, of course, determines when optimum water temperatures for spawning can be expected to occur. In Florida, large-mouths may be on their nests as early as February or March. In Kentucky, their mating behavior may not get underway until

The shallow headwater region of a lake is the first to warm in spring. Spawning activity may not occur in the deeper tailwater region until several more weeks have passed.

May. And in the northern border states and southern regions of the Canadian provinces, the reproduction process may not begin until June. These staggered spawning times from north to south similarly apply to smallmouths and spotted bass.

10. Given the above guidelines, every angler should own a battery-operated water temperature gauge and regularly monitor his/her favorite local waters.

11. Keep in mind that bass spawning activity does not simultaneously get underway in all parts of a given body of water. The shallow headwater region, where feeder tributaries enter the lake, sees the first spawning activity simply because that area warms faster than other sections of the lake. This is where the season's first spawn-fishing activities should be concentrated.

12. The mid-regions of a lake may not warm to spawning temperature for as much as ten days after the headwater area has warmed. And the deepest part of the lake, near the dam, may not warm to suitable spawning temperatures for still another two weeks after that.

13. On any body of water, the northern and northwestern coves, creek arms, and shorelines warm much faster than those areas on the south side of the lake. This is because the northern and northwestern lake areas receive longer daily periods of the

A lake's north and northwestern coves and creek arms are always warmer in spring than coves and creek arms of the same depth on the opposite side of the lake because they receive more sunlight and are protected from prevailing northwesterly winds.

warming springtime sun than other places do. They also are generally protected from the last cold winds of fading winter.

14. Veteran anglers know they have to be versatile when fishing for spawning bass. For example, when you're faced with tough postspawn fishing in a lake's northwestern areas, don't despair. Simply zip across the lake to the other (southern) side where you'll likely find the bass still in a spawning mode. Or motor downlake toward the dam, where you'll likely find bass aggressively feeding in the prespawn stage.

15. If an angler finds tough postspawn fishing in the deeper part of the lake near the dam, he or she should automatically know what to do: Motor all the way to the opposite end of the lake to fish the shallow headwaters where the bass have long since finished spawning and are now following their normal summertime patterns.

16. With largemouths, the spawning process begins with the males being the first to move into the shallows to select nesting sites. How deep they will construct their beds depends upon water clarity and therefore the amount of sunlight penetration; this is because adequate sunlight is required to incubate the eggs

Largemouths spawn shallower than smallmouths and spotted bass. Their saucer-like beds are often visible to the naked eye.

that the female will later drop. As a rule, largemouths spawn at depths ranging from one to five feet.

17. Male smallmouths construct their nests considerably deeper, as the female's eggs don't require as much sunlight warmth to incubate. The average depth of their beds is four to eight feet but often exceeds 15 feet. Fish scientist Milton Trautman has found smallmouth eggs hatching at 22 feet in Lake Whitmore, Michigan.

18. Spotted bass generally construct their spawning nests at an average depth of six to 12 feet.

19. The actual locations of the spawning sites are determined by the bottom composition and wind and wave action. Ideally, look for largemouth bass to be spawning over firm bottom materials such as hard-packed sand, shell, pea-gravel, clay, or marl (loosely packed clay and limestone) with a very thin layer of mud covering the hard material. Largemouths like to sweep out their nests with their tail fins, and the combination of hard bottom materials covered with marginal amounts of soft mire is the best of all conditions for their needs.

20. Prospective spawning sites should be as free as possible from siltation, which is the deposition of finely granulated sediment on the bottom. Small amounts of sediment can be kept in suspension by the continual fanning action of the bass' tails and fins, but too much sediment settling upon the eggs will suffocate them.

21. For every largemouth bed you find along a main-lake shoreline, you'll find ten back in the quiet coves, embayments, and creek arms adjacent to the main-lake basin. If the lake you're fishing has few quiet backwaters and most of your time must be spent working the main-lake shoreline, look for shoreline configurations and cover features that offer protection from wind and wave action. Examples include small cuts in the banks, downwind sides of shoreline points, and shallow stumpfields.

22. Largemouths prefer to nest in such a manner that they can back up against some type of object, or in some type of cul-de-sac, from which they can more effectively defend the bedding site against other fish that will try to eat the eggs or newly hatched fry. When scouting for beds, be alert for logs laying in the water, large rocks, stumps, or standing timber at the water's edge, with the root masses spreading out underwater.

Smallmouths and spotted bass construct their spawning nests at greater depths than largemouths do.

A majority of largemouth spawning activity is done in quiet coves and creek arms protected from wind and wave action. As this aerial photo clearly shows, it's not difficult to determine where most early-spring bass action will be taking place.

23. Although bass do not engage in schooling behavior during the spawning season, they nevertheless may have their beds concentrated rather closely in certain lake regions, simply because ideal spawning sites are usually at a premium. If you find one bed, expect to find others nearby.

24. As a rule, a largemouth's spawning bed is circular, from 12 to 25 inches in diameter, and about six inches deep. In clear water, they're easy to spot because their pale, saucer-shaped depressions contrast with the darker surrounding bottom materials.

25. Smallmouths prefer to construct spawning nests in rather exposed regions, such as wide creek arms and along main-lake shorelines, where mild current or wind and wave action can keep the water aerated. Because of this, it can be quite difficult to spot smallmouth beds: Not only are they often too deep to see, but the constantly moving water prevents them from assuming a nice symmetrical appearance as in the case of largemouths.

26. Spotted bass seldom move into protected coves and embayments to spawn. Like smallmouths, they tend to prefer feeder tributaries

where there is a bit of current, or remain right on the weather-exposed banks of the main-lake configuration, wherever the bottom is gravely, sandy, or scattered with rocks. If there are stick-ups or light brush is present, so much the better.

27. Since smallmouths prefer a rocky, infertile habitat, they commonly fan out spawning nests on stairstep-ledge formations and gravel shorelines. Yet they seem almost nonchalant about nest building and maintenance, often merely dropping their eggs in some handy depression surrounded by shards of rock.

28. Similar to smallmouths, spotted bass are not meticulous in their nest-building and maintenance activities.

29. While male bass are inshore, selecting sites for their spawning nests, female bass stage in nearby deeper-water holding locations, waiting for their suitors to escort them to the nest. In larger and deeper lakes and reservoirs, frequent sites of female largemouth holding stations are sharply sloping points that extend from shorelines and guard the entrances to coves, creek arms, and other quiet backwaters. In the largest reservoirs, with very large embayments that hold bass year-round, female largemouths also may hold along the edges of inundated creek channels winding through the bays.

30. Female smallmouths and spotted bass that are destined to spawn on the main-lake shorelines usually select holding stations at breaks on the first or second breaklines.

31. If you're working the shallows during the prespawn period and you're catching only small bass, they're undoubtedly all males. Begin working the shoreline points, or the breaklines, and you'll likely catch the larger females.

32. Glenn Lau, a famed underwater photographer of bass behavior, says females like to select holding stations that have so-called "rubbing logs." These may consist of not only logs but also stumps and standing timber. According to Lau, females rub against these objects in an instinctive attempt to loosen the eggs from their skeins. This loosening action subsequently allows the females to more easily deposit their eggs in the spawning nests. Tip: When fishing breaklines, points and other female holding stations, concentrate most of your efforts wherever there is timber; if there are no logs, look for boulders.

Male largemouths construct the spawning beds while the larger females wait at the mouths of coves and creek arms. Look for rubbing logs, which the females bump against to loosen their egg skeins.

33. The number of eggs dropped by female largemouths, small-mouths, and spotted bass depends upon the size of the fish. A three-pound bass drops an average of 8,000 eggs.

34. Bass do not feed much during the spawning period, but they can be coaxed into striking at lures and baits. By the type of strike received, an angler can tell in advance whether he's hooked a male or female. Female largemouths on their nests are continually engaging in housekeeping activities to keep the bed clean of debris; if a leaf, twig, or plastic worm drifts into the nest, the female will gently inhale it, swim away several feet and blow it out.

35. Male largemouths on their nests do not feed much during spawning but are very defensive of the bedding site and will attack predators that otherwise will attempt to eat the eggs and newly hatched fry. Lures resembling panfish, snakes, salamanders, or crayfish that are retrieved around the nesting site will consequently draw vicious strikes.

36. Male and female smallmouths, and male and female spotted bass, do not feed much during the spawning period, but they

None of the bass species feed heavily during the spawning period.
They often strike at lures in defense of their bedding areas, however.

do reflexively strike at whatever may be perceived to be intruding into their nesting site. For both species, one of the most popular spawn-fishing lures is a chartreuse-colored, ⅜-ounce jig dressed with a white plastic twister tail.

37. If the water is cloudy and you can't cast to largemouth spawning beds because you can't see them, work the sunny sides of stumps, fallen logs, standing timber, and rock piles that seem to offer suitable bedding sites. If there is a bed there, it will be on the sunny side so that it is exposed to the warming effects of the sun.

38. After depositing her eggs, the female largemouth plays no further role in the egg- or fry-rearing process and gradually drifts away from the bedding site. The eggs hatch from two to five days after they've been fertilized. Although the male remains on the bed to protect the young fry from predation, he eventually succumbs to his increasing hunger and becomes a leading predator himself, gobbling up as many fry as possible. This is Mother Nature's scheme to make the fry scatter into nearby emerging weed growth and begin fending for themselves.

39. Unlike largemouths, male smallmouths and spotted bass abandon their spawning nests shortly after they've fertilized the eggs dropped by the female. As a result, smallmouth and spotted bass mortality rates in the egg and fry stages are always high.

40. Even with largemouths, only three to five percent of the young bass ranging in size from the fry to fingerling stage will survive to adulthood. In a large reservoir that may be 50 miles in length, however, tens of thousands of bass beds may be constructed each spring. Despite the low survival rate of young bass, this is usually sufficient to sustain the fishery.

41. The best words to describe the postspawn stage are "erratic" and "unpredictable." What the angler does at this time may or may not work on a given day. Smaller male bass of all species, now exhibiting voracious appetites, can be caught in the general, former spawning area with a wide variety of offerings. As the weeks go by, look for them to steadily move farther away into heavier cover, deeper water, or both.

42. Larger female bass of all species may remain in their postspawn recuperative phase for weeks. If they can be coaxed into feeding, it's most often with jigs or soft plastic lures presented liter-

For all bass species, the postspawn phase is a resting period characterized by brief flurries of feeding followed by long hours of inactivity. For best results, use a wide variety of lures and work widely separated locations.

ally right in front of their noses. In coming weeks, they too will gravitate toward heavier cover or deeper water, or both, and will begin engaging in more active feeding behavior.

5

40 Habits of Bass That Live in Natural Lakes

Natural lakes offer bass habitat that is more diverse than that found in any other type of water.

Natural lakes are classified by their geological ages. They were formed over the eons by earthquakes, glaciers, and volcanoes.

1. Natural lakes were created long ago by rocky chasms that slowly filled with rainwater and runoff from higher ground, by springs seeping to the surface and filling depressions, by glacial activity and earthquakes, by volcanoes, and by the effects of sinkholing. Many natural lakes are hundreds of thousands of years old.

2. Natural lakes are classified according to their geological ages, and this determines which bass species reside in a particular lake and how they live, move, and feed. Some natural lakes, typically in more northern latitudes, are not capable of supporting bass populations.

3. Scientists have identified and named three types of natural lakes in accordance with their ages. They are *oligotrophic, mesotrophic,* and *eutrophic*. Along the continuum of chronological age, oligotrophic lakes are the youngest. They may, in fact, be thousands of years old, but are considerably younger than mesotrophic (middle-aged) lakes, which are tens of thousands of years old, or eutrophic lakes, which are still older.

1.

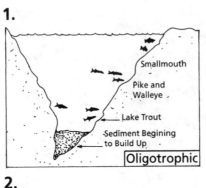

Smallmouth

Pike and
Walleye

Lake Trout

Sediment Begining
to Build Up

Oligotrophic

3. Largemouths and Rough
Fish in Shallow Weeds

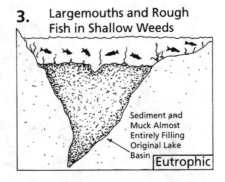

Sediment and
Muck Almost
Entirely Filling
Original Lake
Basin

Eutrophic

2.

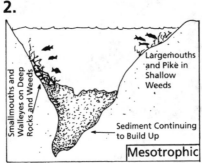

Largemouths
and Pike in
Shallow
Weeds

Smallmouths and
Walleyes on Deep
Rocks and Weeds

Sediment Continuing
to Build Up

Mesotrophic

How Natural Lakes Age Through the Process of Eutrophication

Natural lakes age through the process of eutrophication. As the basin slowly fills in, the water becomes progressively shallower and supports the presence of different fish species.

4. Natural lakes have unique personalities and may age at widely different rates in a process known as *eutrophication*. This involves the gradual filling in of the lake basin by the buildup of decaying plant and animal matter, shoreline erosion, and sedimentation; as a result, the body of water slowly becomes progressively shallower.

5. It's important to understand this aging process of natural lakes because, as a natural lake becomes older, and shallower, certain species of plants and animals begin to vanish since the habitat is no longer conducive to their needs. Other species subsequently take their places. These changes are accompanied by dramatic shifts in the food chain and successive plant life.

6. Oligotrophic lakes are the deep, cold, infertile lakes commonly found in the northern Canadian provinces, and are home primarily to lake trout, walleyes, and northern pike. The only bass found in oligotrophic lakes are smallmouths, and even they do not begin appearing until quite late in an oligotrophic lake's

Eutrophic natural lakes are the most shallow and almost always choked with vegetation. Largemouths are the predominant species, although spotted bass have been stocked in random locations.

life, at about the time the body of water is beginning to reveal the first hints of becoming a very early mesotrophic lake.

7. Finding smallmouths in late-stage oligotrophic lakes is relatively easy because the fish will be in very shallow water (generally, less than 12 feet deep) around shoreline boulders and other rocky cover throughout the year.

8. Eutrophic lakes are shallow, warm, marshy lakes that occur primarily in the middle and southern sections of the country. They are inhabited mostly by roughfish and scavengers such as carp, bowfin, catfish, and gar, and by assorted panfish species. The only bass found in eutrophic lakes are largemouths, and they reside in such lakes only during the earliest eutrophic stages.

9. Finding largemouths in early-stage eutrophic lakes is relatively easy because they will be in shallow water (the depths have long since filled in), usually around weedbeds.

10. Since finding smallmouths in oligotrophic lakes and finding largemouths in eutrophic lakes is easy even for an angler of only average skill, the primary focus of this chapter will be on finding smallmouths and largemouths in mesotrophic lakes; these are the most numerous natural lakes in the contiguous United States. Most are located in the northern border states; they are the most difficult to study and interpret because they contain such a wide variety of bottom structure and types of cover. Just as natural lakes as a group are classified into three age groups, mesotrophic lakes themselves are referred to as being young, middle-aged, or old.

11. Young mesotrophic lakes generally have smallmouths as the dominant bass species, with only a smattering of largemouths, and then only in the shallow embayments. Middle-aged mesotrophic lakes may have both largemouths and smallmouths in relatively equal numbers in a wide variety of locations. And old mesotrophic lakes may have largemouths as the predominant bass species, with smallmouths only minimal in number and found only in the lake's deeper and cooler regions.

12. When bass feeding impulses are triggered, they can be ferocious predators, but they're always at the mercy of the prey they feed upon. Similarly, the prey is highly dependent upon still smaller life forms, all the way down to plankton. Consequently, in natural lakes, all manner of complex interrelationships may exist. If their prey shifts location, for example, bass must follow unless the prey ventures into the habitat niche of some other predator species (such as northern pike). If that happens, the bass generally will avoid the area and begin relating to a less-favored prey item.

13. Understanding the most common predator-prey relationships in natural lakes—indeed, in any body of water—is important because it determines where the bass are most likely to be found at a given time and which lures or live baits are likely to prove the most productive.

14. In familiarizing yourself with the natural lakes in your region, start by talking with a fishery biologist at the local fish and game agency. These biologists monitor the population levels of all fish species in their region's many waters, and can tell you what bass species inhabits a given natural lake and what the predominant forage is.

The postspawn period will often produce some of the hottest largemouth action of the year.

15. The composition and productivity of the food chain in most bass waters varies throughout the year, and has a marked effect on fishing success. During late spring and early summer, for example, the body metabolism of postspawning bass increases dramatically—which often results in good bass fishing. The reason for this is simple: Early in the year the food chain has not yet developed to the point of being abundant enough to satisfy the bass' growing appetite. As a result, the bass are both eager and gullible, and pounce on anything that even barely resembles food (including an angler's lure).

16. As midsummer approaches—when the water is warmest and the bass should be at their hungriest due to their peak metabolic activity—fishing success often seems to fizzle, causing

frustrated anglers to refer to this time frame as the "dog days." Actually, the bass are indeed feeding ravenously, but the food chain has proliferated so rapidly that the bass are now far more selective and cautious. Enormous schools of baitfish, as well as hoards of insects, amphibians and crustaceans, are all active at this time. With so much available food, a bass can simply yawn as an inappropriately chosen lure swims by or a live bait is sloppily and unnaturally presented.

17. After the first few hard frosts of autumn, a fisherman's "luck" once again sees a dramatic turnaround, but for reasons not apparent to many anglers. The cold weather, particularly in the northern states, usually sees a massive die-off of the baitfish populations. Crustaceans and amphibians begin burrowing into bottom muck for winter hibernation. The insects have been largely erased. And young-of-the-year panfish have grown so large that they no longer constitute easy pickings. The only thing that hasn't begun to wind down is the body metabolism of bass. Consequently, as there is again a marked absence of food, the bass no longer exhibit the selectivity that character-ized their feeding patterns months earlier, and they once more become quite responsive to lures or baits.

18. Weeds of various species are found in all waters, from the smallest farm ponds to the largest man-made reservoirs. But

Mesotrophic natural lakes are less fertile than eutrophic lakes. They have less aquatic vegetation and therefore contain both largemouths and smallmouths.

weeds play an especially important role in mesotrophic natural lakes because, in such lakes, largemouths and smallmouths must share the habitat with larger gamefish such as northern pike, chain pickerel, walleyes, and muskies. Since the bass are only an intermediate species, not at the top of the food chain as is usually the case in man-made reservoirs, they instinctively know they may become something else's meal if they roam very much. Because of this, they commonly relate to weeds where they can capitalize upon their predatory advantage of feeding by ambush. At the same time, their almost truncated body shapes allow them to maneuver quickly to elude elongated species such as pike, which are more efficient predators in open water.

19. Anglers should learn to identify the types of weeds bass favor most. State fish and game agencies usually have drawings or photos of the most common weed species in local waters. In mesotrophic natural lakes, bass distinctly prefer one of the three species of cabbage weeds: tobacco cabbage, broadleaf cabbage, and curly cabbage.

In mesotrophic natural lakes, there may be many different types of vegetation favored by the inhabiting predator species. The bass distinctly prefer cabbage weeds, cabomba, coontail, lily pads, and reeds.

20. If cabbage weeds are absent from a particular natural lake, the next most preferred weed species are cabomba and coontail.

21. In mesotrophic lakes, bass may periodically relate to lily pads, cattails, and reeds, depending upon the time of year, the forage they're tied to, and competition from larger predators.

22. Several factors influence the most successful presentation of lures and live baits around weedbeds. Most important is the angle of the sun. If the sun is on your back as you are casting toward a weedbed, its slanting rays will reach far back and underneath the leading edge, and bass on that side of the weedbed will be much deeper within the weeds. But if you cast to the weeds with the sun in your eyes, you'll have much better success; the near edge of the weeds will not be as brightly illuminated, and bass will therefore be closer to the outside edge and more likely to see your offering.

23. When the wind is gusting, bass tend to vacate the weeds and take up positions in open water on the downwind sides of the vegetation, provided larger predators don't pose a threat. The strong wind literally "blows" the baitfish out of their weedbed hiding places into open water, where the waiting bass gorge upon them.

24. In addition to fishing the outside edges of thickly matted weedbeds, don't overlook winding alleys, slots, and potholes. On calm days, bass commonly watch these openings for prey items that may expose themselves. Don't cast directly into the opening, as that may spook the fish. Cast weedless spoons, soft plastic lures, spinnerbaits, and buzzbaits beyond the hole, crawl them to the edge of the hole, then slowly swim them across the opening.

25. Not all weedy locations, even if one of the preferred species predominates there, are attractive to bass; the bottom contour is the key. If there is a long stretch of cabbage weeds, for example, those growing on an irregular, undulating bottom will attract more bass than a spot with an endlessly flat, smooth bottom. In the case of lily pads, if the water is clear, concentrate only upon the largest-diameter pads you can find, as they offer bass the best concealment. If the water is murky or off-colored in some other way, concentrate upon beds of small "dollar pads."

How Bass Relate to Lily Pads

1.

Bad Lily Pads

Weeds growing on irregular bottom contours are far more attractive to bass than those growing on even bottom contours.

2.

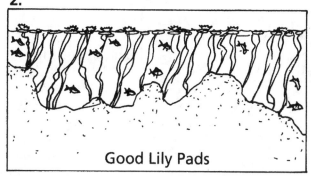

Good Lily Pads

If one type of weed species, such as lily pads, predominates in a given area, the bottom contour will determine which area of the weeds bass will use. They prefer an undulating bottom contour over a flat bottom.

In the case of reeds, bass prefer tight beds of thick-stemmed reeds over sparse beds of thin-stemmed reeds. They also prefer those reeds situated at the edges of drop-offs rather than those located on a flat bottom or tight against the shoreline. One exception is a field of reeds on a flat bottom but far out in an open mid-lake area.

26. Fish only green weeds and avoid brown weeds, which become more common as fall approaches. Brown weeds are an indication that the cover is beginning to decompose and is going into its winter dormant stage. Due to the curtailment of oxygen-producing photosynthesis, the weeds are now releasing carbon dioxide, thus making that area unsuitable to bass.

How Bass Relate to Reeds

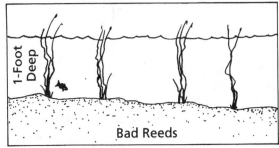

Thin reeds in shallows attract few fish.

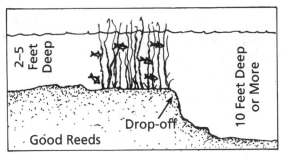

Thick reeds in moderately deep water near a drop-off attract more bass.

Some reed banks may be so expansive that finding bass may seem to be a hit-or-miss affair. Tip: Avoid the shallowest reeds in favor of those in slightly deeper water, and work the outside edges where the depth abruptly drops off.

27. Bass in natural mesotrophic lakes, especially smallmouths, prefer crayfish whenever they are available. They gorge most heavily upon crayfish when they are in their molting, soft-shell stage. In natural lakes that have a high lime content, crayfish molt more often than they do in acidic waters. Lure selection is therefore easier in natural lakes, since all you have to do is study the shoreline. If you see pines and other conifers, and especially cedars, which prefer highly alkaline soil, lure selection is a no-brainer; use crayfish look-alike lures because that is undoubtedly the primary forage the bass are tied to. Conversely, if you see mostly hardwood tree species such as aspens, birch, maples, and oaks— species that don't require such alkaline soil—the crayfish are not molting as often and the bass are consequently relying equally upon various baitfish and minnow species.

When the presence of a large predator species prevents bass from roaming far offshore to forage, they're often found relating to banks of reeds in shallow to moderate depths.

28. In natural mesotrophic lakes where predator species larger than bass are not found in abundance, largemouths and smallmouths are not tied so closely to vegetation. In these waters they are free to roam widely and can be frequently encountered foraging in open water far from the shoreline. In this case, the bass congregate in sometimes amazingly large numbers in and around places where rocky cover predominates.

29. The two predominant types of forage that bass relate to in an open-water, rocky habitat are crayfish and various minnow species. They also like leeches, hellgrammites, and amphibians such as salamanders. Therefore, it pays to carry lures that mimic these forage items as well.

30. Many anglers might think that rocks are rocks, but smallmouths and largemouths distinctly favor certain types of rocks and rock formations over others. First consider the shape of the rocks. The bass may use pea gravel, small round rocks, and large round rocks if little else is available, but these are the least favored.

31. Bass tend to prefer a mixture of small and large slab rocks with sharp angular features, undoubtedly because the numerous crannies provide ideal hiding spots for crayfish.

32. The manner in which the rocks were stacked on the bottom by glaciers and other phenomena also plays a role in bass location. In many mesotrophic natural lakes, the rocks were piled so high on the bottom that, when the basin later filled with water, small islands were created. An occasional largemouth or smallmouth can be taken around such islands, especially during the spring spawning period, but such islands otherwise don't attract great numbers of bass, as food is limited.

33. One exception to the above rule is when two relatively large mid-lake islands are close to each other, separated by a narrow channel of water no more than about 200 yards wide. The time to fish the island channel, which looks like a saddle underwater,

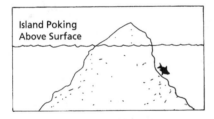
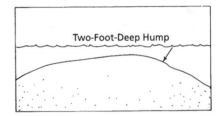
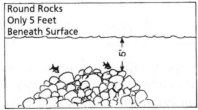
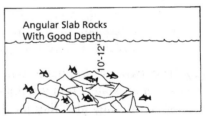

Islands poking above the surface, smooth featureless bottom contours, and round rocks attract few bass. Look for good water depth, angular rocks.

There is an endless variety of rocky cover in most mesotrophic natural lakes, but largemouths and smallmouths prefer certain shapes and configurations. Those rocky formations that are irregular, rather than smooth, and have at least 10 feet of water over them, attract the most crayfish and baitfish and therefore the most bass.

is during midsummer when baitfish numbers are at their peak and on days when the wind is gusting. Strong winds push large schools of baitfish around, and when the wind direction on a given day is just right and pushes the baitfish between the two islands, it concentrates them, as though forcing them through a funnel. Largemouths and smallmouths quickly congregate at the downwind end of the island channel and gorge upon the huge amounts of forage.

34. Far more attractive than islands that rise above the surface are sunken, rock-capped islands, commonly called reefs. These can range in size from no larger than your living room to the size of a football field or even larger. I haven't found any correlation between the size of a reef and its attractiveness to bass, although obviously a very large reef will hold more fish than a tiny one.

35. Those sunken, rock-capped islands that top off at six to 10 feet below the surface, with surrounding water depths of at least 25 feet, are the number-one hotspot that most bass anglers search for in natural lakes.

36. Bass relating to reefs are commonly found in three types of locations. When actively feeding, they may be near the top of the rock-capped island, usually during the low-light hours of dawn and dusk. During midday, as the sun penetrates the water, look for them at deeper levels along the sides and around the

This sonar printout of two sunken, rock-capped islands in a mesotrophic natural lake shows bass relating to the islands, probably foraging upon crayfish. Yet other bass are off the islands, suspended beneath a school of baitfish (the dark crescent).

perimeters of the reef. When resting, or when thrown into a state of inactivity due to a cold front, look for them to gather in pods and to suspend in open water as much as 10 or 15 feet off the downwind side of the reef. Clearly, working this type of structure is where a quality sonar unit pays its way.

37. In natural lakes, another premier location for finding both large-mouths and smallmouths is a point on the shoreline. The most productive ones are those littered with chunk rock and angular rock shards, as opposed to round rocks or gravel.

38. There are two types of points that will attract and hold more bass than others. The first is a very steep-sloping point, where the water depth may drop 25 to 50 feet only yards from the shoreline. Here, bass may forage for crayfish on both sides of the point in calm weather. When the wind is blowing, however, they'll patrol the upwind side of the point for baitfish that have been pushed up and into the V-slot found there.

39. The second type of attractive point is one that tapers gradually, extending far offshore for perhaps 100 yards or more before suddenly dropping off steeply at its tip into water at least 25 feet deep. Bass may forage almost anywhere on this type of point during the early and late hours of the day. When the weather is windy, they'll be positioned off the downwind side, waiting for forage to be blown from the point out into open water. During midday, they may be found either resting or feed-ing just off the steep end of the point.

40. The largest mesotrophic lakes frequently have bass populations that adhere to distinctly different lifestyles: those that live out their entire lives (including the spawning weeks) in close as-sociation to the shoreline; and those that live exclusively in as-sociation with offshore structures throughout the year. If, on a given day, you're not catching fish on shoreline structures and cover, try the offshore structure and you may find the large-mouths and smallmouths there to be more active. Conversely, if the offshore angling is slow, head for the banks.

6

48 Habits of Bass That Live in Man-made Reservoirs

Impoundments that serve the living and recreational needs of millions of people also serve as the homes for billions of bass.

Flatland reservoirs are essentially flooded swamps and bogs and the cover, both above and below the surface, is profuse.

1. In the United States, artificial lakes, or reservoirs, outnumber natural lakes by 100 to 1. In most cases, they're created by building a dam on a flowing water such as a river or large stream and allowing the reservoir to fill by backing up and inundating valleys and other terrain. Although private utility companies and state fish and game departments occasionally create reservoirs, most are created by government agencies for the purposes of flood control, the generation of hydroelectric power, or to supply a local town or city with drinking water. Fishing and other forms of recreation are a side benefit. Nationwide, 1,500 of these reservoirs sprawl over 10,000 acres or more.

2. While natural lakes are classified according to their geological ages, man-made reservoirs, which are created over previously dry land, are classified according to the features of the original landform. The three most common types of reservoirs are *flatland,* *highland,* and *canyonland.* We'll look at them in sequence.

3. Flatland reservoirs are commonly found in the Midwest and South where the topography is level and consistently at or below sea level. When a dam is built, the water backs up to flood stands of hardwood, farmlands, prairies, marshes, lowland swamps, and similar terrain. Most flatland impoundments possess a tremendous

Flatland Reservoir
(Top View)

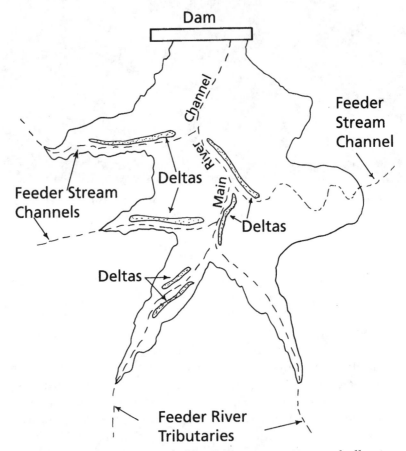

Flatland reservoirs are created by damming a river and allowing water to back up for as much as 50 miles. Most are created for flood control. (Top view)

variety of cover above and below the water's surface. Stumpfields, standing and felled timber, grassbeds, matted expanses of weeds, brush, boggy islands, and other types of junglelike growth may seemingly be everywhere. In other impoundments, cover may be present only in the shallow headwater region and various embayments and creek arms, with the depths near the dam being relatively open water.

Flatland Reservoir
(Side View)

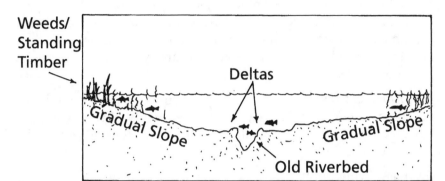

The predominant bottom structure in a flatland reservoir is the old river channel and associated feeder stream channels that dump into it and their deltas (ridges along the edges of the watercourses). (Side view)

4. Most flatland reservoirs are basically shallow, averaging four to 10 feet deep near the headwater region and 20 to 30 feet deep near the tailwater region of the dam.

5. The uniqueness of flatland reservoirs is twofold: First, the deepest water in any region of the impoundment is the bed of the old river that was dammed; and second, although there may be gradual rises or depressions here and there, and occasional ditches found along the edges of inundated roadbeds, the main riverbed and the beds of associated feeder streams that dump into it constitute the major bottom contours.

6. As a rule, largemouths are the principal gamefish species stocked in man-made reservoirs, because of their adaptability to a wide range of water chemistry and terrain conditions. Smallmouths and spotted bass are rarely present in flatland impoundments, but are commonly encountered in highland and canyonland reservoirs, especially if they existed in the original river system.

7. In most cases, flatland reservoirs are also stocked with various combinations of other species such as striped bass, hybrid bass (offspring of mated white bass and stripers), chain pickerel,

catfish, a wide variety of panfish species and, typically, several species of baitfish forage.

8. In a majority of flatland reservoirs, the largemouth is the premier gamefish species and occupies the apex of the food chain. Finding itself in such a situation—under little threat from larger predators—the largemouth is able to roam just about anywhere it pleases; of course, this behavior is always in accordance with its water-chemistry requirements.

9. In flatland reservoirs, individual bass may be caught randomly almost anywhere that natural or man-made cover exists, but schools of bass are usually found only in the vicinity of the riverbeds.

10. Bass living in flatland reservoirs exhibit spawning behavior that's similar to those living in natural lakes; their water temperature preferences and nest-building activities are the same, so the angler's lure selection and lure presentation should be similar as well.

11. One major difference worth noting is that flatland reservoir bass spend the deep winter in the main riverbed and, when spring arrives, although they may leave the riverbed and fan out randomly on nearby flats, they more commonly follow associated feeder stream channels into large embayments or swamps. This, then, is the most important key to finding spring bass; check your topo map to find embayments that have "active" stream channels running through them as they will contain far more fish than other embayments that are simply catch basins for rising water levels during rainy periods.

12. Two other types of spawning locations are notable. One is an old roadbed, which is most often comprised of hard-packed sand or gravel (there may even be concrete or asphalt roads with a light covering of silt that has settled from the water). And the other is an abandoned railroad spur left intact when the reservoir was flooded. Both features are usually marked on maps; if not, the shoreline may reveal where they enter the water, and you can trace their routes with sonar equipment.

13. Spawn-spent bass usually retreat into the nearby stream channel depths they followed into the shallows. Concentrate your lure presentations in and around cover lining the channel and, as the weeks wear on, progressively follow the stream channel

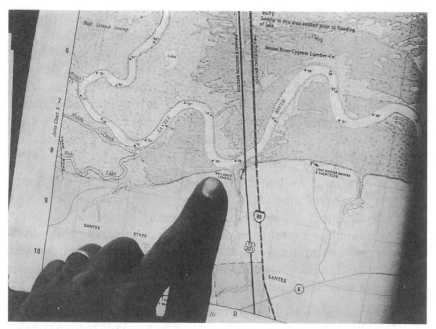

One flatland reservoir hotspot for bass is a channel point where the old river bed loops in close to a shoreline point. Bass congregate in channel point areas in summer and winter.

to the mouth of the embayment as the bass will be slowly gravitating back toward the main-lake basin.

14. One hotspot among bass and bass anglers alike is a channel point. This occurs where the old riverbed loops in close to shore and a tapering point of land simultaneously extends all the way to the edge of the channel.

15. Another place where bass congregate is on a delta. These are elongated ridges sometimes found along the edges of stream channels and riverbeds. They're found predominantly in regions of former agricultural operations, having been created by farmers plowing bottomlands right up to the edges of streams and rivers, and generally are covered with stumps, trees, and brush.

16. Carefully studying a topo map may also reveal junctions where two stream channels join. This situation gives birth to underwater points, ridges, saddles, humps, and similar features that are highly attractive to bass.

17. In addition to natural features, flatland reservoirs customarily have an abundance of man-made features that attract and hold bass. During the hot summer months, I scan my topo map for old farm ponds which now, if they're on open flats, serve as "holes" that bass retreat into to escape the overly warm water. Old building foundations on the bottom, bridges (now underwater) that cross tiny streams, and the rocky rubble or "riprap" in causeways (highway foundations) that border or cross flatland reservoirs are also attractive to bass.

18. Many flatland impoundments, especially those in the South, have extensive amounts of shallow swamp habitat. Most have wide expanses that are virtually impenetrable due to fallen logs and standing timber; the predominant species are cypress, willow, sweetgum, tupelo, and black oak. Likewise, there are sure to be huge fields of matted weeds; the most favored by bass are elodea, hyacinth, hydrilla, milfoil, lily pads, and moss.

19. Many bass anglers like to slowly fish through junglelike cover, casting randomly to targets that look bassy. This method works, but you'll have greater success if you focus on standing timber and weeds that are close to the edges of stream channels where the water depth drops off abruptly.

20. The best time of day to fish a swamp is high noon. When the sun is directly overhead, the extensive vegetation releases more oxygen into the water than at any other time, and this invigorates the food chain. Microorganisms and insects exhibit heightened activity, which stirs baitfish and panfish into activity, causing bass to respond.

21. Because the primary purpose of most flatland reservoirs is to facilitate flood control and the related drainage of terrain upstream from the impoundment, water levels are adjusted to accommodate rainfall. Typically, rain-swollen feeder tributaries gush into the reservoir and the water level slowly rises until it reaches its predetermined holding capacity, whereupon the gates of the dam are opened and the water level is allowed to slowly recede. In many cases, the dam gates are opened ahead of time in anticipation of heavy rainfall. The best bass fishing takes place when the water level is slowly rising. Under these conditions, bass (both schools and stragglers) begin migrating into the shallows and are far more aggressive and responsive to lures. Some anglers believe this is due to the sudden availability of additional

When a flatland reservoir is periodically drawn down to kill weed growth or so that maintenance work may be done on the dam, many features are exposed. This old country bridge is usually under 10 feet of water. A smart angler who marks its location on a map will have a hotspot that few others know about when the lake is allowed to refill.

food. Conversely, when the water level is falling, fishing action generally takes a nosedive. The bass move deeper than usual, into temporary holding stations, until the water level stabilizes. They can still be caught at this time, but you'll have to work very hard for them.

22. Occasionally—perhaps once every five years or so—the agency that manages a flatland reservoir will dramatically draw down its pool level. This is usually done to expose broad shallow areas and kill off weeds that have grown to the point of hampering boat traffic. It's also done to allow maintenance work to be performed on the dam, highway causeways, and private docks and breakwaters. Whenever a lake is drawn down and much of the bottom is exposed, search for bottom structures that you didn't know about and mark them on your map. When the reservoir is allowed to refill, you'll have bass hotspots that other anglers don't know about.

When this flatland reservoir was drawn down, a wide creek arm revealed these two parallel, wooded ridges. When the water level is raised to its former level, the flooded timber may hold plenty of bass.

23. Highland reservoirs are found in hilly or mountainous regions. They are usually made by building a dam between rather steep mountain ridges and permitting river water to back up and flood associated gorges and valleys.

24. A highland reservoir rarely has much weedy cover, except perhaps along short stretches of shoreline, in the backs of coves and embayments, and in the headwater region. The weed species are usually moss, lily pads, cabbage, and milfoil. Standing timber, however, may be profuse from one end of the lake to the other; this normally consists of cedars, pines, and various hardwoods.

25. Unlike the mucky floor of a flatland reservoir, the bottom of a highland reservoir is usually hard and clean, consisting of sand, gravel, rock, silt, or a combination of these materials. Lacking the rich, fertile bottom materials that give flatland reservoirs a variety of water colors, highland impoundments are generally clear, although they frequently take on a milky or pale green color after a heavy rain.

Highland Reservoir
(Top View)

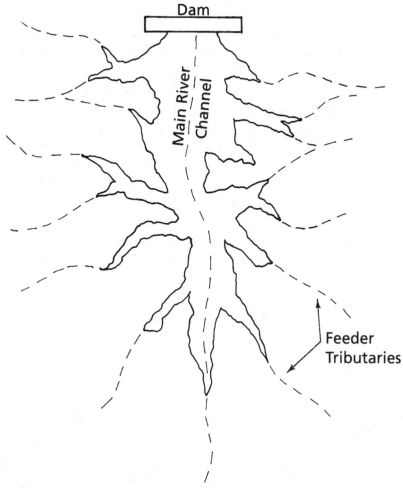

Highland reservoirs are created by building a dam between two steep mountain ridges. Instead of sprawling over a wide area, the reservoir is typically long and narrow, with many creek arms and jagged shoreline features. (Top view)

26. Also unlike flatland reservoirs, largemouths are not the only bass species found in highland impoundments. In many cases you'll also find equal (or even greater) numbers of smallmouths and spotted bass. Other gamefish may include striped bass, walleyes, muskies and, in some cases, northern pike. When a

larger predator species is present, particularly northern pike or muskellunge, highland reservoir bass behave similarly to those in natural lakes.

27. A wide variety of panfish species, plus a combination of baitfish species such as threadfin shad, gizzard shad, various shiner or minnow species, and in some cases smelt or herring, are also found in highland reservoirs.

28. While bass in flatland reservoirs use the inundated riverbed and associated feeder stream channels, such is not the case in highland reservoirs. These reservoirs typically reach depths of 200 feet or more, making most of the old river channel simply too deep to be used by bass. Even many of the feeder stream channels toward the tailwater (dam) region may be too deep. This causes bass to be closely tied to the shoreline year-round.

29. The shorelines of highland reservoirs are usually steep and sharp-breaking. Bluffs, cliffs, sheer rock walls, and similar features often cause the water to plummet to 50 feet deep or more

Highland Reservoir
(Side View)

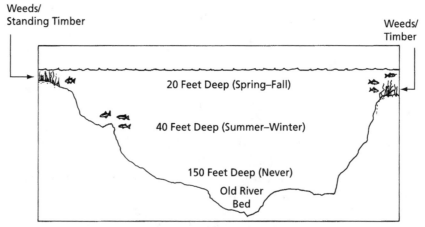

In a highland reservoir, bass generally locate in either spring/fall locations that are less than 20 feet deep, or in summer/winter locations that are up to 40 feet deep. The only time they are occasionally found in mid-lake areas is during the fall, when they suspend beneath schools of baitfish swimming on the surface. (Side view)

The Bass Angler's Almanac

just yards from shore. Underwater, there are typically ledges, outcroppings, and other rock formations of endless description that stairstep down into the depths.

30. It has been estimated that as little as 10 percent of the water in a highland impoundment is suitable bass habitat. Because of this, it's much easier to find and catch bass in a highland reservoir than in a flatland reservoir, where bass can roam widely.

31. During the spring spawning period, look for largemouths to travel up into the feeder tributaries almost as far as they can go to find suitable shallow water; they may also select spawning sites in shallow, weedy, or brush-choked coves or embayments. Smallmouths and spotted bass generally prefer to spawn on shallow shelves covered with sand or small patches of pea gravel along the shorelines of the main-lake basin.

32. During summer and winter, highland reservoir bass spend a good deal of time suspending at mid-depths. This most often occurs along rock walls near shore or off ledges or rock outcroppings. To catch bass in these situations, anglers commonly hug the steep shoreline walls with their boats, and cast parallel to them. The method is called "stacking" the lures, and it involves first casting a lure that runs three or four feet deep, then switching to a lure that dives to the six- to 10-foot level, then switching again to an offering that runs 12 to 15 feet. Once you determine the level at which the fish are holding, continue to fish at that depth.

33. In summer and winter, bass also suspend in standing timber close to shorelines. Now, either flip jigs into the crowns of the trees and work them up and down at various depths, or vertically fish jigging spoons from top to bottom. No matter where bass may be suspending—whether in timber or along rocky shorelines—an LCD sonar or graph recorder can make finding the fish, and the depth where they're holding, much quicker.

34. In fall, bigger largemouths, smallmouths, and spotted bass tend to remain in the standing timber or near the shorelines. Smaller bass, averaging from 1½ to 2½ pounds, commonly school up and roam mid-lake regions, looking for schools of surface-swimming baitfish which, in turn, are following wind-blown masses of plankton. The bass travel beneath the baitfish at depths generally ranging from six to 10 feet and periodically rush to the surface to slash into the forage. This creates a churning, surface carnage, often an acre or

Locating bass in a highland reservoir is easy because only 10 percent of the impoundment is suitable bass habitat. The rest of the water is too deep.

The Bass Angler's Almanac

more in size which, if the surface is calm, is sometimes visible from a half mile away. If you spot such frenzied feeding behavior, race to the location and cast baitfish-look-alike lures into the melee.

35. The "jump-fishing" action discussed above is usually brief, no more than five minutes in duration, after which the bass go back down to their previous level beneath the preyfish and continue following them. While bobbing at rest in mid-lake, use binoculars to scan for surface-feeding action that may be too far away to detect with the naked eye. Also be on the alert for flocks of water-oriented birds (gulls, terns, kingfishers) that suddenly appear and begin swooping down to the surface. Such birds keep track of the baitfish schools, and they dive to the surface to pick off the bait when feeding action is underway.

36. The water level in highland reservoirs is usually manipulated several times daily to create hydroelectric power. The water level of the entire reservoir may come down only a fraction of an inch, but the current that's created triggers bass into feeding activity. If you look at the surface of the water very closely, especially in the creek arms, focusing upon bits of leaves and other debris, you'll even see it traveling slowly in a downstream direction, even though the dam site where they're pulling water may be 30 miles away. Many anglers like to check with the

Jump-fishing occurs on highland reservoirs when bass charge into surface schools of baitfish. The tip-off that such carnage is underway is seeing water birds swooping and diving to the surface to pick up bits and pieces of shad.

Since highland reservoirs are created for flood control purposes and the generation of hydroelectric power, water levels are regularly drawn down, causing bass to relocate to cover or bottom contours previously too deep for them. By using a depthfinder, you can find these bottom features and use floating markers to outline their dimensions.

impoundment's managing agency to learn exactly when they pull water each day, and then plan to be on hand during those peak feeding periods.

37. Highland reservoir pool levels are commonly drawn down semi-permanently during the winter in anticipation of spring snowmelt and rainwater. This drawdown is far more dramatic than when generating electric power. Sometimes the water level is brought down 20 feet or more and allowed to remain at that level for four or five months. At first, the receding water level turns bass off and they retreat into deep holding areas. However, once the water level has stabilized, action begins to pick up again. You may have incredible fishing success during this time, since the fish are more concentrated now than at any other time.

38. The bass in highland reservoirs may achieve hefty sizes, but the extreme water clarity in some of these impoundments dictates that you use lighter lines and smaller lures than you would fish on flatland reservoirs.

39. Canyonland reservoirs are located predominantly in the western and southwestern states, where mammoth concrete dams

Canyonland Reservoir
(Top View)

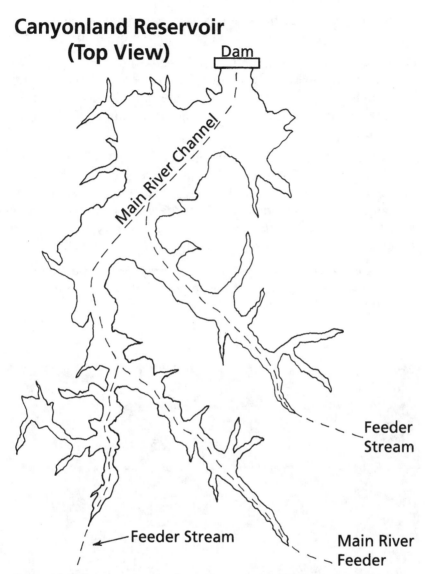

Canyonland reservoirs are long, narrow, and have many creek arms. The water at the dam may be as much as 600 feet deep. In the spring, look for bass spawning in the creek arms or on shallow, silt-covered benches along the main-lake shoreline. (Top view)

span relatively narrow gorges and rushing rivers are allowed to back up and inundate vast networks of deep chasms. Such impounds are generally created to produce hydroelectric power and drinking water for large metropolitan areas. The water depth near the dam may be as much as 600 feet, and water level fluctuations during power generation periods and winter drawdowns may range from 10 to more than 150 feet.

40. Typical bass cover in the form of weeds and standing timber is virtually nonexistent in a canyonland reservoir, although sparse swatches of sagebrush, manzanita, mesquite, scrub oak, juniper, and cottonwood trees may occur, particularly in the backs of coves.

41. Largemouths are the predominant bass species, although the Florida subspecies and smallmouths have been introduced into some waters. Their favored forage is shad and crayfish. In many canyonland impoundments where there are Florida bass, however, a "two-story" fishery permits them to gorge upon young rainbow trout, which are found in colder, deeper water.

42. Bass in canyonland reservoirs are closely tied to the shorelines because the remainder of the impounded water is simply too deep and cold for them.

Canyonland reservoirs are very deep chasms designed to generate hydroelectric power and to hold large quantities of drinking water for desert communities.

The Bass Angler's Almanac

Canyonland Reservoir
(Side View)

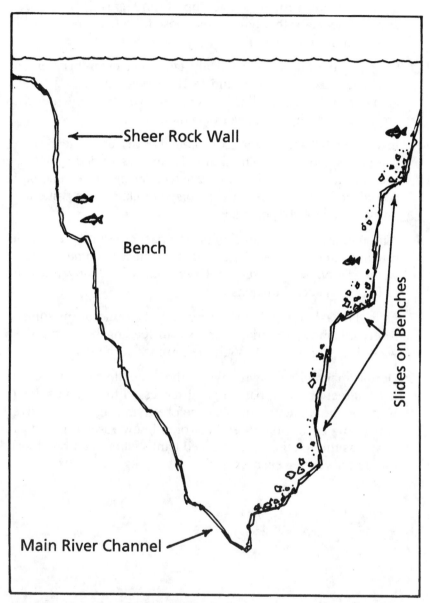

In summer, fall, and winter, look for bass against the main-lake shorelines where there are deep benches, rocky outcroppings, and talus slopes (gravel slides). (Side view)

43. With the exception of the small amounts of woody cover that may be present, the shoreline regions bass favor most are composed of rock walls, ledges, shelves, and slides. Slides are slanting underwater structures made up of sand, gravel, chunk rock, and boulder slabs that have come loose from the canyon's walls and fallen into the water.

44. Spring spawning activity usually takes place far back in the shallowest areas of coves and feeder creeks. It can also occur along main-lake shorelines where relatively shallow benches are covered with a thin layer of sediment.

45. In summer, fall and winter, bass locate themselves on steep shoreline points, along shoreline drop-offs, and suspended against the sheer facings of steep walls, occasionally rising or descending in accordance with the presence of forage or changes in water temperature or sunlight penetration.

46. Although the locations of canyonland bass are quite predictable, catching them can be difficult due to the sometimes extreme water clarity. Long casts, spiderweb lines, and tiny lures are called for in such situations.

47. As in the case of highland reservoirs, bass found in canyonland reservoirs show a marked increase in feeding behavior when water is being pulled through the turbines at the dam.

48. During major drawdowns, when the water level may quickly fall 100 feet or more, bass angling success virtually shuts down. Wait for the water to stabilize before trying again. Moreover, you'll now be fishing an entirely brand new reservoir, and can treat it as though the now-exposed banks where you previously caught bass never even existed.

7

40 Habits of Bass That Live in Rivers and Streams

How to consistently catch bass in moving water.

All three species of bass are present in many rivers and streams, but they'll predictably be in different locations.

1. River fishing opportunities, particularly for bass, are far more diverse than those found in most lakes and reservoirs. Quite often, all three species—largemouths, smallmouths, and spotted bass—can be caught in a single day, sometimes in almost the same location.

2. Smaller rivers and streams are rarely home to overly large bass, but hook a two-pound smallmouth on an ultralight spinning rod

Most anglers don't think of river bass growing to large sizes. But keep in mind the 22-pound world-record largemouth came from an oxbow of the Alabama River, as did these six-pound smallmouths.

with 4-pound-test line and it feels like you're tied to a runaway bus. As for larger rivers, the world-record 22-pound 4-ounce bass was caught in an oxbow of the Alabama River; need we say more?

3. Bass in rivers and streams, like those in lakes and reservoirs, use shoreline features, bottom contours, and cover such as weeds and wood. But there is one additional condition found in waterways that is not found in lakes and reservoirs on a 24-hour basis, and that is current.

4. Current has certain irrefutable characteristics, no matter where the river or stream is located. For one, a current is always stronger just below a dam or rapids and for a few miles downstream, until it gradually begins to diminish in velocity. As a general rule, the current of any flowing waterway will usually be much stronger toward the surface and toward the middle of the flow. Lesser current velocities are usually found along the floor of the river or stream and close to the banks.

5. Moving water always takes the easiest route, until some land feature diverts it, creating a bend. In time, the current washes

One feature of all rivers and streams is current, which greatly influences bass holding stations and the presentation of lures.

out and undercuts the outside bend, making the water much deeper there. Conversely, the inside of the bend has a quieter flow of water, which allows sand, gravel, and sediment carried by the current to settle to the bottom and create a shallow bar or shoal.

6. In flatland areas, a river or stream may be straight as an arrow for mile after mile. But in hilly or mountainous regions, or places where there are mixtures of soft and hard ground, perhaps with occasional rocky terrain, look for a river to take on a serpentine form.

7. In smaller rivers and streams, bass of all species, but especially largemouths, try to avoid the waterway's strongest flows. They commonly do this by resting in depressions scooped out of the bottom, letting the fast water rush above them. They may also rest behind the protection of mid-stream boulders, allowing the current to be diverted around their holding positions. Or, they may cling to shoreline locations where cover formations either block the current (such as where felled trees along the banks lay partly in the water) or where terrain configurations (such as indentations and cuts) create quiet pockets of water.

In smaller rivers and streams, bass commonly seek protection by clinging to shoreline cover. In large rivers that are relatively shallow, they may also live in midriver locations where bottom obstructions block the current flow.

Wing-Dams
(Top View)

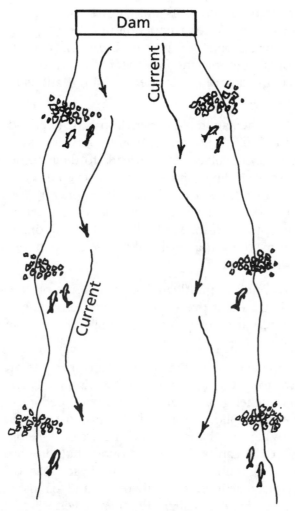

The purpose of wingdams is to prevent shoreline erosion by shunting the current toward the middle of the river channel. The velocity of the current determines whether bass will be on the front sides of the wingdams, on the outermost tips, or on the protected back (down-current) side.

8. In larger rivers, bass also relate to protective shoreline features. But in large rivers that are relatively shallow, they also live in mid-river locations, seeking areas with reduced current velocity on the down-current sides of islands and wingdams.

9. No matter what the velocity of the current, bass always face directly into the flow, as this allows them to maintain their positions with the least expenditure of energy. It also allows them to watch for food passing by in the current. They may have to dart out into the fast water to capture a prey item, but they will quickly return to their holding stations in the quieter edge waters.

10. Because of the nature of their environment, river and stream bass usually look different from lake and reservoir bass, which generally enjoy a sedentary life that leads to their becoming chunky and pot-bellied. River and stream bass, even those living in sluggish waterways, must continually burn energy just to maintain their positions in the moving water. As a result, they develop long, lean, torpedo-shaped bodies and a well-toned musculature that can make even a smaller-than-average fish feel like a racehorse when hooked.

11. One exception to the "lean and mean" rule of river-bass physiology is bass that live in unique river environments, such as long feeder arms of quiet water that are far from the river's main course.

12. Bass populations inhabiting rivers and streams are extremely sensitive to changing water levels. Spring rains, snowmelt runoff from higher ground, and the influx of feeder tributary water may cause smaller rivers and streams to swell far over their banks. When this happens, and the water is rising slowly, the fishing action can be fantastic around shoreline bushes, brush, and standing timber. Bass move into these areas to feed upon a wide variety of insects, earthworms, and panfish and baitfish that are feeding on smaller prey themselves.

13. When water levels begin to slowly recede, bass gradually drift back to their former holding stations. However, if levels begin dropping abruptly, look for most angling action to terminate. This often happens when the rising water begins seriously flooding adjacent shoreline regions and a managing agency, perhaps many miles downriver, opens the dam's floodgates—which can

Bass inhabiting rivers and streams typically fight longer and harder than their lake counterparts because their muscles have been strengthened by battling the current.

cause the water level to drop 10 feet or more in just a few hours. Once the water level stabilizes, the bass action will begin to slowly increase.

14. Large rivers can sometimes be fished in the same manner as flatland and highland reservoirs. There will be current to contend with, but there will also be similar depths and bank features. However, bends—which may be fish magnets in smaller rivers and streams—generally aren't, in themselves, prime bass habitat in larger rivers. In rivers such as the Ohio, Missouri, and Mississippi, a bend may well be a mile long and several hundred yards wide.

15. In a majority of cases, big-river bass orient themselves either to the river's shorelines or feeder tributaries. The main river channel itself is usually too deep and swift to attract bass. The bottom of the channel may even be featureless, the result of being scoured clean by dredges to facilitate barge and tugboat traffic.

On the largest, deepest rivers, the bottom generally lacks features to attract and hold bass. In these waters, most of the fish relate to cover on shoreline shelves or are found in the river's feeder tributaries.

16. On a large river, bass tend to hang along shoreline shelves along the main channel in summer, fall, and winter. These features, quite common on rivers used for interstate commerce, appear as narrow benches extending out from the bank perhaps 20 yards before dropping off sharply into the main channel. Such structures are attractive to bass of all species because of a combination of desirable features: suitable water depth ranging from three to 15 feet; close access to much deeper water if necessary; the presence of a long, abrupt breakline; and an abundance of breaks on that breakline, in the form of logjams, driftwood, stumps, boulders, and similar cover, which attract baitfish, panfish, and crayfish.

17. In a large river, bass spend the spring and early summer weeks in the numerous tributaries feeding into the main river channel. Typically, the shorelines of such creeks and small rivers are lined with trees, stumps, rocks, and weedbeds. Since such tributaries are never dredged, the bottom may have holes, bars, rockpiles, and similar fish-attracting structures, allowing the angler to fish the water in the same manner as he would a natural lake or flatland reservoir.

18. At the conclusion of their spring and early summer spawning activities in a large river's feeder tributaries, bass begin to drift back to the main river channel to congregate on the shoreline points at the mouths of the main river channel and along its associated shoreline shelves.

19. In the Deep South, where year-round bassing can be enjoyed on large rivers, wintering fish generally use the same types of main river channel shelves as during the summer and fall, only at somewhat deeper levels. The markedly cooler water during winter calls not only for deeper-running lures, but for much slower lure speeds as well.

20. In a large river, whenever the water on a shelf is less than six feet deep, and especially if the current is moderate, the recommended lures for largemouths and spotted bass are spinnerbaits, crankbaits, and plastic worms. For smallmouths, go with crayfish-look-alike crankbaits, jigs, and baitfish-look-alike crankbaits. If the water is more than six feet deep, or if the current is moving swiftly, these lures will be carried far out of position before they've had a chance to get down near bottom where the fish are holding. In these cases, switch to heavier jigs or jigging spoons for all three species.

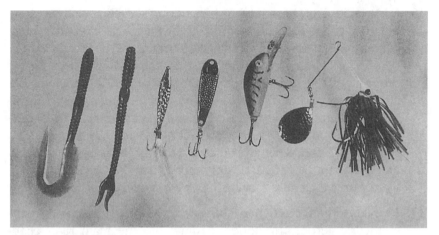

On large rivers, the same types of lures used in flatland and highland reservoirs are fine. But if there is a swift current, make sure you also have lures that are heavier than usual or can be weighted.

21. Sandbars, gravel shoals, and clamshell beds are common on large rivers that are shallow, possess a rather sluggish current, and are not used for interstate commerce. These bottom features are usually elongated in shape and quite similar to the deltas that exist along the edges of inundated river channels in flatland reservoirs. They're especially attractive to schools of baitfish and, therefore, largemouths and spotted bass. But a swift current caused by a torrential rainstorm can erase a sandbar overnight. Then, after the rains have abated and the current has moderated, a new bar may begin forming somewhere else.

22. The best time to fish such mid-river structures is when the current velocity is slow to moderate. One popular method of fishing these mid-river features is to motor slightly upstream of the bottom structure, let out live minnow baits on weighted lines, and drift over the top of them. Make as many drifts as necessary to thoroughly check the entire structure.

23. Another popular technique of fishing mid-river bottom features is called "river-slipping." Instead of free-drifting a long distance, anglers use their outboards or electric motors to hold them in position to fish the structure thoroughly with crankbaits or jigs. In this technique, the throttle speed is set just a tad slower than

OxBow
(Top View)

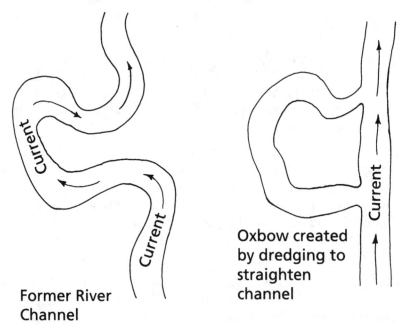

Current

Current

Current

Former River
Channel

Oxbow created
by dredging to
straighten
channel

*A common feature on large rivers used for interstate commerce is
an oxbow created by dredging to eliminate sharp turns in the river
course. What's created is a quiet backwater that can be fished just
like a eutrophic natural lake or flatland reservoir.*

the current velocity so the boat is not continuously maintained
in the same exact location, but has a tendency to "slip" back a
few feet at a time.

24. A feature unique to many large rivers used for interstate commerce is an oxbow. This is a place where a former loop or S-turn
in the river channel has been straightened out by dredges to
facilitate barge traffic. The result is the formation of a crescent-
shaped backwater that possesses little or no current. Since the
shoreline shelves are littered with stumps, brush, and standing
timber, and since the absence of current also encourages the

emergence of lily pads and cabbage weeds, most oxbows can be fished in the same manner as a highland reservoir.

25. Since there is little or no current running through an oxbow, yet a profusion of cover and plenty of forage, bass quickly begin to take on the same chunky, pot-bellied characteristics as their lake-bred brethren.

26. The one disadvantage of oxbows is their unpredictable accessibility. Most times, there will be a narrow cut leading into an oxbow from the main river channel, and another cut exiting; these cuts are usually open to small-boat traffic, but during low-water periods they can be reduced to bare trickles.

27. Most rivers and their feeder tributaries have a variety of man-made features that attract bass. Examples include docks, rubble "riprap" protecting banks close to roads, and concrete pilings supporting bridges and railway trestles. When the current is sluggish, the bass may be positioned almost anywhere around these features, but if the current has a moderate to swift velocity they'll always be on the protected downcurrent side.

28. Many rivers have wingdams just below their main dams and downstream for perhaps a half mile. These are man-made structures of cribbing and natural materials, usually logs and railroad ties interspersed with boulders. Since the current's velocity just below a dam at various times can be very swift, wingdams extending 20 to 50 yards out into the river help to shunt the main flow of the current toward the middle of the river, thus preventing the banks from seriously eroding. When the current is strong, bass will hold in the deep, quiet water close to the shoreline on the downstream side of the wingdam. When the current begins to moderate, they'll move away from the shoreline a bit, and also begin climbing somewhat up the backside of the wingdam toward its crest. When the current is light, they may be at the very tip of the wingdam, adjacent to the main river channel, on top of the wingdam, or even in front, upstream facing the structure.

29. Very small rivers, streams, and creeks may meander through rural farmlands, black-bottomed swamps, woodland tracts, or deep rocky gorges. North of the Mason-Dixon line, smallmouths are the dominant residents, but in the South they may hold a combination of smallmouths and spotted bass, depending upon the

Many rivers contain man-made wingdams just below their main dams. These structures are made of rocks and timber, extend varying distances out into the river channel, and at a given time may hold all three species of bass.

elevation. Since smallmouths require cooler water temperatures and a stream gradient of at least 3 percent, they are most likely to inhabit mountain creeks or spring-fed lowland streams. Spotted bass tolerate somewhat warmer water, and inhabit nearly all streams and creeks ranging from 1,000 feet in elevation to below sea level. Largemouths are generally bonus fish in these waters, since they need still warmer temperatures and a gradient of less than 2 percent.

30. Though not common, finding all three species of bass in the same water does occur in some small rivers, streams, and creeks. They'll usually be in distinctly different locations, with the smallmouths closer to the edges of the current than the spotted bass, and the largemouths in the slowest glides and on the downcurrent sides of protective cover and shoreline features.

31. Bass rarely form schools in small rivers, streams, and creeks, although widely separated deep pools may hold loose groupings of fish during midsummer and in winter. Otherwise, in a majority of cases, the fish are loners.

32. It's rare for most small rivers, streams, and creeks to produce bass exceeding two or three pounds. Such waters simply don't produce enough food, so competition among the predators for the available prey is fierce, with much of that food-intake spent on using energy against the current.

33. Stream and creek bass primarily feed on small crayfish, hellgrammites, crickets, grasshoppers, locusts, and small minnows. The

The forage base is small in small rivers and streams, so always downsize your lures. These offerings are adequate representations of the minnows and dace species found in most small rivers and streams.

Should you fish upstream or downstream in a creek or stream? There are advantages and disadvantages to both, but most anglers fish upstream so their lures or live baits will travel naturally with the current flow.

best all-around lures are therefore ¼-ounce jigs in brown, black, or olive colors, slim-minnow plugs, and straight-shaft spinners. Small spinnerbaits also come in handy for fishing weedy areas.

34. Should you fish small rivers and streams in an upstream or downstream direction? If you fish in a downstream direction, you have to be careful not to dislodge gravel, silt, and other debris when wading or maneuvering your craft through shallow riffles, as this can tumble downstream through areas you intend to fish next and spook any bass that are present. On the other hand, you may inadvertently stir up crustaceans, nymphs, and other tasty tidbits that will drift downstream and may cause bass to start taking a greater interest in any potential food items—including your lures—that suddenly come their way.

35. The main disadvantage of fishing upstream is that one must almost constantly be paddling in order to make forward progress or even maintain a given position; if the water depth allows for it, a small outboard or electric motor solves this problem. The great advantage of fishing upstream is that, since bass always

face into the current of any flowing waterway, the lures you cast upstream, and then retrieve, will be traveling downstream and look more natural.

36. In the spring, all three bass species have little alternative but to find spawning sites along the banks, many times only yards from the main current. Think "protection" and look for fallen trees along the shoreline where the trunk is in the water, providing a quiet nesting location. Or, search for jumbled shoreline boulders that form a bowl of sorts, or areas where the bank is undercut, or places where trees standing at the water's edge have large root systems that extend out from the bank.

37. In the spring and fall, bass in small rivers, streams, and creeks usually relate to the current but find areas where they are protected from it. Let's say there is a large boulder in the middle of the creek. On the upstream side, the current is forced to split around the rock. Right where the current splits, particulate matter in suspension will have settled out and piled up, but directly behind the rock there is almost invariably a depression. Either a largemouth or spotted bass may select this place as a feeding station. Approximately five to 10 yards downstream of the rock, the two tendrils of diverted current join and the water appears bubbly or mildly turbulent. Expect smallmouth action if there is any bottom feature, such as rubble, at this junction.

38. Another hotspot for smallmouths is where two streams join, or where a still smaller creek enters the main flow of a stream.

39. If the small river, stream, or creek is off-colored because of recent heavy rainfall, it will be difficult for an angler to see below-surface rocks, logs, and other obstructions that may be serving as holding stations for bass. The key is to watch the surface of the water and any drifting bits of flotsam, twigs, leaves, or even foam. If a twig or leaf suddenly deviates to the left or right from its straight downstream drift, then a rock or log below is diverting the current. If the debris seems to hesitate, or briefly sweeps back upstream, it is being influenced by swirling eddy water, which indicates a quiet pocket directly below and some obstruction on the bottom just a few yards upstream. A large boil on the surface indicates a very large underwater obstacle, such as slab rock.

40. The largest bass (of all species) that one is likely to encounter in a small river, stream, or creek come from sweepers located in

the longest and deepest pools. Generally, the fish will be holding right in the middle of the sweepers when the current is mild, dropping back to the far downstream side as the velocity increases. Many anglers like to take a position upstream of the sweeper and, using lures or live baits, slowly pay out line incrementally, allowing the current to take the offering into the maze of branches. Stronger-than-usual-pound-test line may be required to muscle a hooked fish out of the cover.

8

40 Habits of Bass That Live in Farm Ponds and Strip-Mine Pits

Tiny waters offer fast action with big fish, and in many cases you don't even need a boat.

Don't overlook farm ponds and strip-mine ponds. Eighty percent of all state-record bass have come from bodies of water smaller than 50 acres.

1. According to the National Sport Fishing Foundation, in the past 20 years 80 percent of all state-record bass have come from bodies of water smaller than 50 acres in size. Many of these fish have tipped the scales at eight to 14 pounds.

2. According to the Department of the Interior, at last count there were more than 6 million "fishable" farm ponds dotting the countryside, with more being created every year.

3. Most farm ponds are created for the purposes of watering live-stock, to supply drinking or irrigation water, or strictly for recreation. Most are privately owned and trespass permission must be gained through the landowner. Generally, the state's fishing regulations do not apply on such waters (check your regulations booklet), although the landowner may impose his own restrictions.

4. In the majority of cases, the bass species stocked in farm ponds are largemouths. Only in New England and across the northern border states do landowners occasionally stock smallmouths as well.

5. As a rule, topo maps are not of use in learning the bottom contours of farm ponds, simply because in the creation of such waters bulldozers obliterated the former land contours.

6. If you want to learn what the bottom contour of a farm pond looks like, the landowner may be able to provide valuable information. Ask where the deepest water is, where the shallowest water is, and whether stumps, tree crowns, tree trunks, boulders, and other debris were left in the basin during the pond's creation. Study the landform surrounding the pond; if it's steep, the pond

Most farm pond bass are largemouths, although in some New England states smallmouths may also be present. Spotted bass don't do well in such waters.

will be like a miniature highland reservoir. On the other hand, if the surrounding terrain is level the bottom will be more like a flat-land reservoir.

7. Some farm ponds are created by simply building a dam between opposing hillsides and allowing the basin to fill with runoff and snowmelt from higher ground; as a result, unless tree stumps and other cover were left intact, the bottom is generally featureless. In this case, the bass will closely relate to shoreline cover such as weedbeds, rock slides, points, and fallen trees lying partly in the water.

8 Most farm ponds are created by building a dam not only between opposing hillsides but also by blocking a creek or stream, thus allowing water to back up; as a result, a main bottom feature will be the old winding stream channel. The largest of these farm ponds may even have smaller feeder tributaries that join

Common Farm Pond Configuration (Top View)

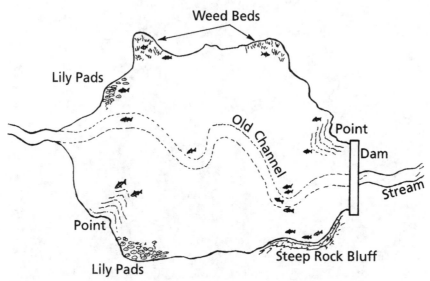

Topo maps are not helpful for studying a farm pond's bottom contour because the terrain was likely graded with a bulldozer. Talk to the landowner who was present when the pond was built, and draw your own sketch. This one is typical of most farm ponds.

Many farm pond owners plant cover on the bottom. The most common are discarded Christmas trees and bundled saplings that are sure to attract bass within days.

with the major stream channel. Bass in these ponds will relate to shoreline cover but also to the twists and turns of the stream channels on the bottom and the stumps and brush cover that typically line their edges.

9. Landowners commonly "plant" additional cover such as discarded Christmas trees in their farm ponds. The standard procedure is to bundle together discarded trees and drag them out onto the ice during winter. Several concrete blocks are tied to the trees, and when the ice melts in spring, the trees sink to the bottom. In the South, where ponds don't freeze over, trees are anchored on the bottom along the shoreline or transported offshore by boat.

10. A pond covering more than five acres, and which has depths to 15 feet or more, is most effectively fished with either an inner tube or a small johnboat with an electric motor. A small, portable sonar unit will also give you an advantage.

11. A relatively shallow pond covering less than five acres is most effectively fished from the shoreline to avoid spooking the fish.

The smallest ponds are most effectively fished from shore, as a boat looming overhead would spook many of the bass.

12. Before fishing, determine whether the pond possesses predominantly flatland or highland characteristics. If it's a flatland pond, the bass can generally spawn anywhere in the spring, even near the dam; they'll spend the rest of the year randomly relating to the pond's cover and bottom features. If it's a highland pond, the bass will generally spawn at the shallow, feeder tributary end of the pond; as the water warms in summer and then cools in fall, they will spend much of their time at the dam end of the pond, relating to cover and bottom features.

13. Farm ponds that have exceptionally clear water and little cover often provide the best bass fishing action after dark.

14. When fishing a relatively small farm pond from shore, sneak cautiously to the water's edge in a crouched position and use bushes and tree trunks to conceal yourself. An angler who boldly tramps right down to the water's edge in a fully erect position will send sound vibrations into the water and cause his silhouette to loom against the skyline; both are sure to alarm nearby fish.

15. The most efficient technique for working small farm ponds from the shoreline is fan-casting in a clockwise direction. Make the first cast to your immediate left, tight against the shoreline, and then radiate each succeeding cast around the clock. Since each succeeding cast will be progressively farther from the shoreline, where the water is sure to be deeper, allow your lure to sink deeper before beginning the retrieve; you may even want to have two pre-rigged rods, one with a shallow-running lure such as a spinnerbait or plug and the other with a deep-working lure such as a jig or Texas-rigged plastic worm. After you've made your fan-cast, hike down the shoreline a short distance and repeat the procedure. If the landowner has built a small dock or pier, don't immediately walk out on it to fish; do that later, after you've stayed back some distance and cast lures to its edges and underwater support pilings.

16. When working a larger, deeper farm pond from a boat, the same techniques apply that would otherwise be appropriate when fishing a flatland or highland reservoir. Simply look at the pond as a downsized version.

17. The same lures and live baits that may be used in flatland and highland reservoirs are equally effective in farm ponds. Just keep in mind that a farm pond's forage base is never as diversified

Farm pond bass commonly relate to shoreline cover, so don't tramp loudly down to the water's edge. Sneak down quietly and try to stand behind shoreline cover when making casts.

Fan-Casting Lures
(Top View)

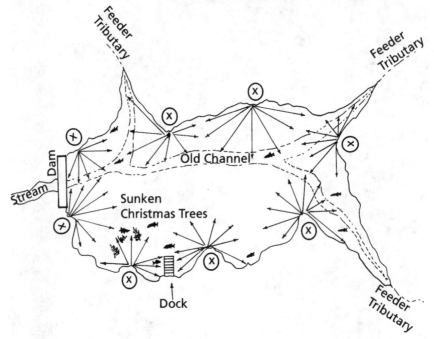

The most thorough way to fish a small farm pond from shore is by fan-casting lures from one vantage point, then moving down the bank 30 yards and repeating the effort.

as that found in reservoirs. If the only forage stocked by the landowner is bluegills, a bluegill-look-alike plug may outfish all other lures by 10 to one.

18. According to the Department of the Interior, there are an estimated 800,000 strip-mine pits nationwide, with more being built each year.

19. Largemouths are the predominant bass species stocked in strip-mine pits, and fish weighing over 10 pounds are occasionally taken from such waters. Only in scattered locations throughout New England and across the northern border states are small-mouths stocked as well.

20. All strip-mine pits are the result of excavating coal. When the mining activity is finished, the site is allowed to fill with water.

Many of the same types of lures that work well in highland and flatland reservoirs are also suitable for farm pond work. Try to closely match the predominant forage base, which in many farm ponds is the bluegill.

The majority of pits are open to public fishing with trespass permission not required; in some cases a daily use permit (usually free) is required so that fishing pressure can be monitored. Although the mining company still owns the land and its ponds, management of the fishery is relinquished to the state's department of natural resources, which studies each pond's water chemistry and stocks fish. The fishing regulations are generally the same as on large public lakes, reservoirs, and rivers.

21. Those states that have the greatest number of strip-mine pits are Arkansas, Kentucky, Illinois, Indiana, Iowa, Kansas, Minnesota, Missouri, Nebraska, Ohio, Oklahoma, Pennsylvania, Tennessee, Virginia, West Virginia, and Wisconsin.

22. Ohio has the largest number of strip-mine pits at the American Electric Power Recreational Area located in the southeastern part of the state. Here, sprawling over parts of three counties, there are currently 580 strip-mine ponds of varying sizes.

23. As their name implies, strip-mine pits are where shallow seams of coal are excavated. The craters gouged out of the terrain are generally rectangular or ribbon-shaped and usually bordered on at least

one side by a high wall. There are exceptions, such as triangular- or square-shaped strip-mine ponds, but most appear as long, narrow fingers encompassing anywhere from one to 50 acres.

24. After the mining activity is complete, the excavation sites are allowed to fill with natural rainwater runoff. Only rarely will you find a feeder tributary entering a strip-mine pond.

25. The strata in which coal seams are found are generally infertile, consisting mainly of sand, shale, slate, and soft rock formations such as sandstone. The resulting strip-mine ponds characteristically reveal exceptionally clear water, at least compared to man-made flatland reservoirs created by inundating marshlands, river bottoms, bogs, or swamps. This infertility prevents an abundant growth of algae, plankton, phytoplankton, and other forms of zoological life.

26. Generally, the only vegetation found in strip-mine ponds are those which are acidic-water tolerant, such as lily pads and coontail moss, and then only in widely scattered locations. The moss in particular is attractive to bass because it forms large, matted, floating blankets that are ever shifting in their shapes as the wind direction rearranges them. Bass like to suspend at arbitrary mid-depths under these canopies, especially during summer. The trick is fishing the side of the mossbed opposite the slanting angle of the sun, which offers the greatest shade.

27. A relatively high percentage of strip-mine ponds are so acidic that they can't support any form of plant or animal life. These are known as "hot ponds." Be sure to check with the agency that manages the fishery in the strip-mining region you wish to fish to learn which ponds are hot, and mark them on your map.

28. When asking the managing agency about hot ponds, also be sure to mention you're specifically interested in bass fishing; in larger strip-mine ponds, the main predator species may not be bass but northern pike, chain pickerel, or channel catfish.

29. A large variety of fish-holding features can be found in strip-mine pits, but some common structures are found in many. The high wall bordering such waters is very similar to the sheer rocky bluffs, gravel slides, shale outcroppings, and ledge-rock formations typical of highland and canyonland reservoirs, with the water depth dropping off very steeply at the edge of the shoreline. The opposite facing bank may be another high wall, but

more frequently it will be a gradually tapering flat. Therefore, fish movements by the seasons are similar to those in other waters, with bass predominantly using the shallow, gradually sloping banks in spring and then shifting to the steeper banks for the remainder of the year.

30. One end of a long, narrow strip-mine pond is likely to be quite shallow and, underwater, feature a ridge that slopes down and bisects the pond lengthwise. This ridge is the old tote road formerly used by dump trucks that backed down into the excavation site, where steam shovels loaded them with coal. Bass will use this structure year-round, in spring for spawning at its shallowest end and then for feeding at progressively deeper levels as the season wears on.

31. The opposite end of a strip-mine pond will have a dam-like structure spanning two opposing hillsides. This originally was the old haul road that the dump trucks used to exit the excavation

Strip-Mine Pond
(Side View)

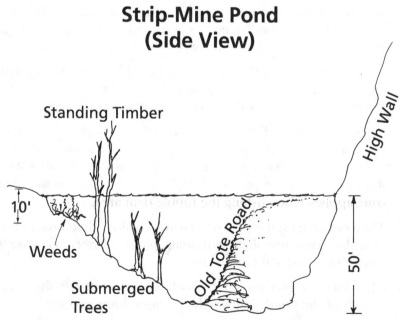

As a rule, strip-mine ponds are deep and have a high wall on at least one side. There's also sure to be an old tote road on the bottom, which is like an underwater ridge. There may also be standing timber and weeds.

region, and now serves as a dam, impounding the water. If the side of the dam facing the water is made of "rip-rap," expect it to be a bass hotspot during summer, fall, and winter.

32. Much of the remainder of the pond floor may be as much as 50 feet deep and therefore not favorable to bass. But elsewhere, in random locations, there may be features that attract and hold individual bass or small pods of fish. Examples include isolated large boulders, rubble or slag piles, and entire trees knocked down by bulldozers and pushed off to one side. Standing timber is also likely to be present—not only trees poking well above the surface, but also those standing in very deep water. By peering into the clear depths, an angler can often see their crowns.

33. As a rule, the managing agencies of strip-mine pits allow boats on only the largest ponds and, even then, outboards are usually prohibited. Many anglers use the same lightweight cartop boat and electric motor they use on large farm ponds.

34. When fishing small strip-mine ponds from the shore, be extremely careful in your footing. Particularly along the high wall side, where the water is deepest, loose gravel or shale comprising the bank is prone to slippage.

35. Since the water in a strip-mine pond is so transparent, the best action typically takes place during the low light levels of dawn and dusk, when the skies are overcast, and after dark.

36. When bass are on the high-wall side of a strip-mine pond, they may suspend at arbitrary depth levels. Stack-cast your lures with crankbaits that run at different depths to strain the water and determine their preferred depth level on a given day. The same applies when fishing the rubble dam area.

37. When bass are on the opposite-facing, shallow shoreline and relating to cover, use shallow-running plugs, spinnerbaits, weedless spoons, and soft plastic lures.

38. When bass are on the old tote road that descends into the deepest part of the pond, use weighted plastic lures and jigs.

39. If you can fish from a boat, and there is standing timber and submerged tree crowns, the best technique is to vertically pump jigging spoons up and down at various depths; the bass' preferred depth level will usually be from eight to 20 feet.

Small strip-mine ponds, less than five acres, are best fished from the shoreline. Stack your lures along the high wall to determine the depth level the bass are using.

Strip-mine ponds can range from one-half to 100 acres in size. A small boat is required to effectively fish the largest waters. Since strip-mine pond water is exceptionally clear, make longer than usual casts.

40. Due to the exceptional water clarity, many strip-mine anglers may logically think in terms of lightweight mono lines. However, due to the abundance of heavy cover, many fish will predictably break off. You're better off selecting a high-strength, thin-diameter line in either a clear or pale-green color.

CHAPTER
9

37 Ways That Water Chemistry and Temperature Influence Bass Behavior

What's in the water makes a big difference to all three species of bass.

1. Largemouths, smallmouths, and spotted bass are relatively tolerant of minor fluctuations in water chemistry and water temperature. But moderate changes in their environments will cause them to fall into a state of inactivity, and major changes will cause them to either leave the immediate area or perish.

2. Rivers and streams, assuming they are not polluted by industrial chemicals or metropolitan waste, seldom see radical changes in water chemistry that might adversely affect bass, since the current homogenizes all elements to a relative uniformity.

3. Lakes and reservoirs, particularly the largest ones, where miles of shoreline twist and turn to form numerous channels, bays, and coves, frequently find themselves subjected to wide variations in water chemistry.

4. It was 25 years ago that Texas A & M University bass researcher Dr. Martin Venneman, using sophisticated water analysis equipment, determined that at any given time from 50 to 80 percent of the water in any large lake or reservoir does not contain enough oxygen to support fish life.

5. Today, small, portable, battery-operated oxygen-monitoring equipment is available to anglers through fishing-tackle mail-order houses such as Cabela's and Bass Pro Shops. The angler lowers a probe attached to a wire line into the water to various depths, and then reads an indicator dial on the face of the instrument. Oxygen-monitoring equipment does not guarantee you will consistently be able to find or catch bass. It does guarantee you will not waste time fishing where no fish can possibly survive.

6. Optimum oxygen levels for largemouths and spotted bass range from 5 to 13 parts per million (ppm), though they highly prefer and will seek out water with 9 to 12 ppm oxygen. Smallmouths prefer somewhat less oxygenated water, in the range of 3 to 8 ppm. Bass of any species that remain in a lake area where the oxygen level is below 3 ppm will die of asphyxiation. And if they remain in areas with more than 13 ppm, they will experience oxygen poisoning.

7. On man-made reservoirs, it's not necessary to be concerned about oxygen levels in the spring because numerous feeder creeks and river tributaries continually pour in large quantities of fresh oxygen-rich runoff water.

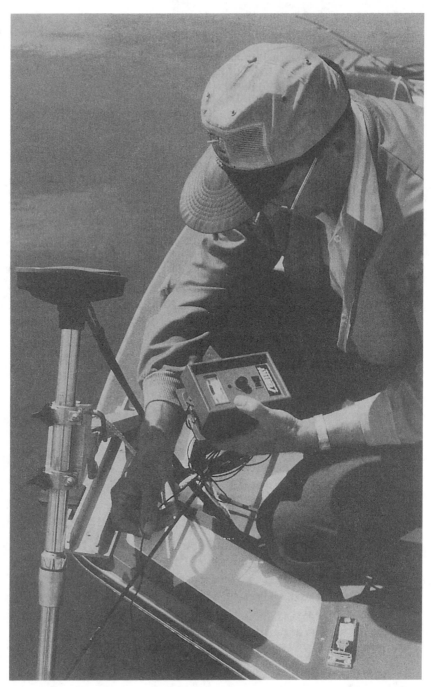

More than half the water in a given lake does not contain enough oxygen to support fish life. Using an oxygen monitor will guarantee you won't waste time fishing where no bass can live.

Smallmouths can exist at lower oxygen levels than largemouths and spotted bass.

8. In large lakes and reservoirs, fluctuations in oxygen levels most often occur in summer and early fall due to abrupt changes in barometric pressure, and wind direction and velocity. The effects of oxygen depletion or oversaturation may last for only a day or two, or they may last for several weeks.

9. Many anglers, before they cast a single lure, motor around and take oxygen-level readings in many locations, jotting them down on their maps. They then concentrate their efforts on those regions where oxygen levels are optimum.

10. During the summer, many bodies of water with depths of at least 50 feet become separated into three distinct layers. This stratification is most common on large mesotrophic natural lakes, highland reservoirs, and canyonland reservoirs. It does not occur on eutrophic natural lakes, flatland reservoirs, farm ponds, stripmine pits, or in rivers and streams.

Representative Reservoir Showing Random Levels c Oxygen Saturation   (Top View)

Since oxygen levels vary from week to week, serious anglers test random lake locations before deciding where to fish.

Representative Lake and Reservoir Stratification
(Side View)

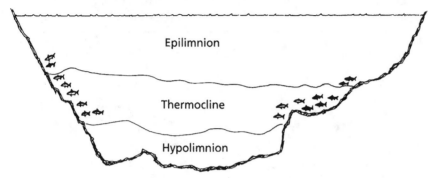

During the summer, deeper bodies of water stratify into three distinct layers. The top two layers are oxygen rich, but the bottom layer is devoid of oxygen. Bass tend to congregate in and near the middle thermocline layer where there is a distinct water temperature change.

11. Of these three layers of water, the deepest layer, just above the lake floor, is called the *hypolimnion*. It's almost completely devoid of oxygen.

12. The middle layer of water is the *thermocline,* and the uppermost layer is the *epilimnion*. Although the upper epilimnion is usually rich in oxygen in most lake regions, the thermocline is even more oxygen-saturated because it is both deeper and colder.

13. What separates the epilimnion from the thermocline is a rapid change of temperature, often as much as 0.5°F or more with each foot of depth. Most thermoclines average seven to 10 feet thick, are found at depths of 20 to 30 feet, and range in temperature from 60° to 70°F.

14. In a lake or reservoir that has stratified, bass will often be found in greater abundance, exhibiting greater activity within the thermocline than elsewhere. The reason for this is that the upper epilimnion layer usually has so much light penetration that bass activity is discouraged, and the bottom hypolimnion is usually devoid of oxygen. That leaves the thermocline, where there is a

REPRESENTATIVE THERMOCLINE BREAKDOWN
IN A HIGHLAND RESERVOIR

Depth (feet)	Temperature (degrees F.)
Surface	78
5	78
10	78
15	75
20	73
25	66
30	60
35	59
40	58
45	58
50	54

The temperatures at 20, 25, and 30 feet (73, 66, 60) are bracketed and labeled "Thermocline."

Most thermoclines average seven- to 10-feet thick and on a water-temperature gauge look like a hovering blanket, where the temperature changes as much as ½° to 5°F with each foot of depth.

favorable combination of reduced light penetration and abundant oxygen.

15. None of the three layers of water are uniform. From day to day they vary in shape and depth, hovering like water-soaked blankets and shifting in accordance with wind and wave action.

16. A so-called oxygen inversion is the occasional, brief formation of yet another layer of water below the oxygen-void hypolimnion.

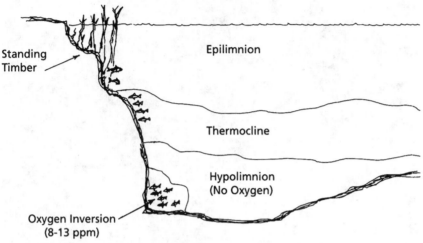

Representative Oxygen-Level Stratified Layers in a Lake or Reservoir (Side View)

Standing Timber

Epilimnion

Thermocline

Hypolimnion
(No Oxygen)

Oxygen Inversion
(8-13 ppm)

An inversion pocket is sometimes created at the bottom of the hypo-limnion. This is an isolated, oxygen-rich area that can concentrate bass in great numbers.

An oxygen inversion layer is usually high in oxygen (8 to 13 ppm) and is most often found near a sharp drop-off or in association with underground springs. Bass may be trapped in an inversion pocket, usually in a fairly confined area, until wind and wave action causes the inversion layer to dissipate; the bass can go nowhere because venturing out of the inversion pocket would mean entering the oxygen-void hypolimnion and perishing.

17. On any large lake or reservoir, only a limited number of oxygen inversions may be in existence at a given time. If an angler stumbles on to one of these hotspots, however, he or she often can expect to catch a bass on every cast.

18. On a daily basis, bass of all species are influenced by the pH of their watery environments. The pH of a solution is a measure of its acidity or alkalinity. The pH scale runs from 0 to 14, with a measurement of 7 considered neutral; anything lower than 7 is acidic and anything higher is alkaline, or basic.

19. All fish must maintain a certain chemical balance in their blood and body fluids if they are to survive. More than two decades

Dr. Loren Hill was the first bass scientist to develop a pH-profiling method of finding bass. A pH level that is too low or too high is toxic to bass; they prefer to locate themselves in lake locations and at depth levels where the pH ranges from 7.5 to 7.9

ago, Dr. Loren Hill, then chairman of the Zoology Department at the University of Oklahoma, developed a device that allowed anglers to measure a water's pH. Since the pH of a bass' blood is slightly alkaline—about 7.6—they seek out water close to this pH value; they're somewhat adaptable, however, and can survive a pH range of 6.7 to 9.6. Given a choice, if there is water within their immediate region that has a pH of 7.5 to 7.9, that is where they will be. When the water pH is within this range, bass are best able to withstand stress, utilize the oxygen in the water, and obtain maximum metabolic value from their food intake.

20. Today, small, portable, battery-operated pH monitoring devices are available through fishing-tackle mail-order houses such as Cabela's and Bass Pro Shops. The angler lowers a probe attached to a wire line to various depths and then reads a dial on the face of the instrument.

21. Checking the water's pH level in various lake and reservoir locations does not assure an angler that bass can be successfully caught there, but it does assure that time won't be wasted fishing where bass are not likely to be. PH devices are also extremely helpful in deciding which strip-mine ponds to fish, as many are too acidic to support any type of vegetation or aquatic life.

22. Some anglers believe that bass have preferred water temperatures that they will seek out, but this is not entirely correct. Rather, there are certain water temperature ranges in which they exhibit the greatest activity levels. Since fishing success depends in large part upon finding active bass, every angler should have a water temperature gauge. They're inexpensive, portable, battery operated, and available through fishing-tackle mail-order houses and tackle shops.

23. In the spring, sunlight slowly warms the surface of the water. Many anglers mistakenly refer to this as the "spring turnover," but the water doesn't really turn over. Since it has a lighter density than the colder water directly beneath, it stays right on top. The only way deeper water is able to warm up is by conduction, the downward transfer of heat from one molecule to another. This warmer water invariably is found in a lake or reservoir's north and northwest sections, which receive longer exposure to the sunlight each day and are usually protected from strong winds.

24. In the spring, if you have more than one lake or reservoir to choose from, remember that a clear body of water will warm much faster than one of the same size that contains off-colored

Representative pH Profile of a Reservoir (Top View)

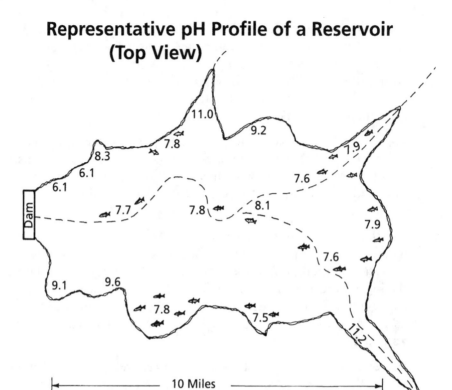

With a hand-held pH gauge, a serious angler can quickly check lake locations to find areas preferred by bass and to avoid areas where fish are unlikely to be.

water. It's a simple physical principle that sunlight can penetrate clear water more easily than it can milky, sandy, or muddy water. Shallow bodies of water also warm more quickly than deeper ones; this is why savvy early season anglers first begin fishing farm ponds, often just days after ice-out.

25. Target your bass species in accordance with the prevailing water temperature. Largemouths are most active in 70°F water, spotted bass in 65°F water, and smallmouths in 60°F water. On a given fishing day, in a reservoir that contains all three species, you may therefore find the fish in different states of activity. If your target species is largemouth bass, you may find them highly active in the shallow headwater section of the lake but lethargic and inactive in the mid-lake and tailwater sections where the temperature is colder.

Hand-held water-temperature gauges help anglers home-in upon a bass' preferred temperature range at different times of year.

In addition to a hand-held water-temperature gauge for checking deeper water where bass are likely to be summering in a thermocline layer, many anglers also like to have a console-mounted gauge in their boat. This gauge monitors the surface temperature and is an aid in finding spring-spawning and fall-turnover areas.

26. In the fall, a genuine turnover does occur. As the surface water slowly cools, its molecular structure becomes denser and heavier, causing it to sink to the bottom. As a result, the warmer, lighter water lying beneath is forced to the surface, is subsequently cooled, and the cycle repeats itself.

27. The fall turnover brings about many changes in the former stability that characterized lakes and reservoirs during summer.

Any thermocline that may have previously existed is quickly destroyed. For a brief period, the water temperature is fairly uniform at all depths. And the water itself may reveal a temporary turbulent coloration as silt, sediment, and decayed organic matter is swept up and circulated.

28. Bass react to the fall turnover by exhibiting behavior that's as unpredictable as the daily changes in the water. The circulating water now homogenizes everything so that water chemistry (oxygen and pH levels) and water temperature no longer restrict the fish to certain areas. The fish may be widely scattered in different locations, at different depths, and associating with different types of cover. The successful angler is invariably the one who is willing to cover a lot of territory during a day and try a wide range of lures and presentation methods.

29. As winter approaches and the water cools to the point where bass activity virtually shuts down, one location that can still provide good bassing is the warm-water discharge from a shoreline industry. Here, the water temperature may be as high as 70°F, resulting in a high level of bass activity in the immediate vicinity; conversely, the water temperature may be only 40°F only 200 yards away, with the bass there being almost comatose.

30. The color, or clarity, of the water in any given natural lake, man-made reservoir, river, stream, farm pond, or strip-mine pit is a condition that can greatly influence an angler's success in catching bass. It determines how shallow or deep the bass are likely to be, the ease or difficulty they have in capturing food or striking at lures, and subsequently which tackle may be most appropriate.

31. Stable water colors, which remain pretty much the same year-round, are a result of the water's chemistry and the physical composition of the bottom materials. In the rockbound, infertile natural lakes of the far North, the canyonland reservoirs of the desert Southwest, the highland reservoirs of the Midwest, and strip-mine ponds, the water is typically quite clear. Conversely, southern flat-land reservoirs and farm ponds, which are nearly always in highly fertile regions, may have a variety of water colors ranging from cloudy green (the result of algae bloom) to brown/black or stained (the result of tannin being released into the water by decomposing brush, felled trees, and standing timber).

32. Stable water-color conditions also result from the presence of certain types of clay or iron ore deposits, which leave the water with

a distinct red or rust color. Very shallow waters with soft mire bottoms (such as eutrophic natural lakes) may take on a muddy brown color throughout the year. Rivers, creeks, and streams that wind through flatland regions of soft terrain may remain brown or sandy colored year-round due to the current keeping sediment in suspension. Creeks and streams cascading through steep, rocky terrain may be crystal clear, on the other hand.

33. Unstable water colors, which often persist only for a short time, may catch the angler entirely off guard. These are caused by high winds, heavy rains, runoff from higher ground, or increased current velocities, all of which roil the bottom sediment. Unstable water colors are nearly always muddy brown or cloudy.

34. The best bass fishing success generally occurs in waters that are slightly murky, milky, or stained. Under these conditions, where bass are not overly spooky, an angler can use heavy tackle if existing cover conditions warrant it, and bass will frequently be found in very shallow water.

35. Sparkling-clear water with a preponderance of heavy cover is the most difficult of all to fish. In such water, bass generally stay deeper than usual, are more easily spooked due to the transparency of the water, and catching them usually requires very light lines and small lures.

36. On the largest bodies of water, an angler should have little difficulty finding the water color that he wants to fish. If the headwater region of a man-made reservoir is too muddy, simply explore other areas downlake toward the tailwater region of the dam. If the coves and bays of a natural lake are roiled, fish the main-lake shorelines or offshore bottom structures.

37. One prime place to find bass after torrential rainstorms is some type of edge, where you can see a distinct change in the water color, usually where muddy or cloudy water adjoins clear water. This mud-line is frequently along the main banks of the lake, several yards out from the shoreline, where wind and wave action created by a recent storm lashed the shallows. It may also be where a small rushing feeder stream dumps into the lake or reservoir. In either case, the newly created edge is a type of structure along which bass like to position themselves, gaining an advantage over baitfish that suddenly find themselves exposed.

Water color often determines where bass are located and what types and colors of lures are most likely to be effective in catching them. One hotspot always worth fishing is an edge where two different water colors meet.

CHAPTER
10

30 Ways That Weather
Influences Bass Behavior

*Just because bass are cold-blooded creatures
doesn't mean they're immune to Mother
Nature's whims.*

1. Bass are extremely sensitive to abrupt changes in their environments. They like stability, but that doesn't necessarily mean calm, settled weather. It refers to consistency in the weather.

2. Bass are most active, and anglers are the most successful catching them, after a three-day stable weather pattern has been in effect. It doesn't matter whether it's dry or rainy, windy or calm, sunny or overcast, hot or cold. What's important is not the specific character of the weather, but the fact that the particular type of weather occurs without interruption for at least three consecutive days. This allows bass time to acclimate themselves to the changes in their environment that developed with the new weather pattern, and to begin a slow and steady recovery to their former levels of activity. Beginning with the fourth day, the fishing should be terrific and it should stay that way until such time as the weather abruptly changes again.

3. Some stable weather patterns seem to result in greater bass activity than others. Most serious anglers pray for a soft but steady rain. Pleasure-boat traffic sharply declines at such times, and other anglers who are not so dedicated to their sport stay home; the bass habitat is consequently not greatly disturbed. Also, an overcast sky and raindrops pelting the surface diminish underwater light intensity, thus making bass feel more at ease all day long, instead of only during the hours of dawn and dusk. This is especially important on lakes that have very clear water.

4. Falling rain also adds oxygen to the water, which has an energizing effect on the bass's body metabolism. Biologists say that rain (and the associated effects of wind) changes the pH of the water by pushing, pulling, rearranging, and homogenizing various layers of water and lake regions, so fish are more inclined to move and become active rather than remain inactive and holed up in isolated places.

5 The number-one weather phenomenon that shuts down bass activity and results in unsuccessful fishing outings is the cold front, which is defined as a line on a weather map that indicates the leading edge of a mass of cool weather advancing into some other region presently occupied by warmer weather. The difference in air temperature on each side of the front may be as much as 25°F.

Cold fronts, with dawn bringing bright, clear skies, are the nemesis of bass anglers everywhere. Most of the fish go into deep water or heavy cover and become inactive.

6. Just before a cold front enters a given region, there is usually a significant upsurge in bass feeding activity. The reason for this is that an advancing weather pattern destined to collide with a resident weather pattern of greatly varying air temperature invariably gives birth to—you guessed it—rain!

7. Many anglers mistakenly reason that the cold air associated with a cold front shuts down bass activity, but that's not the case, as it can take weeks of consistently cold weather to change the water temperature even a few degrees. Rather, the movements, activity levels, and behavior patterns of bass are affected by the trailing edge of the cold front. This edge is characterized by extremely clear and bright skies. Keep in mind that the leading edge of the front is characterized by skies that become increasingly overcast with storm clouds, causing the bass to become more active. Then, suddenly, as the front passes through, the skies clear and there is a significant increase of intense sunlight penetration into the water.

8. The essence of a cold front's influence upon bass behavior is a shock effect not unlike the way moviegoers wince when they first emerge from a dark theatre. Bass likewise react to this shock effect and find themselves confused and disoriented. Their instinctive reaction is to seek the perceived safety of dark or shaded water. Some of the fish accomplish this by diving for the depths and then lethargically lying on the bottom; this is usually the case in highland and canyonland reservoirs, mesotrophic natural lakes, and strip-mine ponds. Other bass bury themselves beneath heavily matted surface vegetation or within the crowns of trees or brush on the bottom; this is usually the case in flatland reservoirs, eutrophic natural lakes, and farm ponds.

9. Fishermen who are locked into regimented schedules, with little flexibility in when they can pursue bass, can still hedge their bets. Say it's Friday night and you plan to fish all day Saturday at a lake 30 miles west of your home. You tune in a weather forecast and learn that a cold front is moving in your direction and should arrive sometime during the night. In this case it would be foolhardy to follow through with your original plans because you'd be fishing post-cold front conditions and have little success. It would be smarter to pick another lake to the *east* of your home. Many expert anglers who know that weather characteristically moves across the country from west to east

commonly drive eastward 50 miles or more, with some particular lake in mind, so they can fish in rainy weather under cloudy skies, at the leading edge of the cold front.

10. If there's no flexibility in your choice of lakes to fish—let's say you're on vacation and have rented a lakeside cabin for the week—consider switching to another bass species. If you've come for largemouths, try instead for smallmouths or spotted bass if one or the other also inhabits the same body of water. The latter two species generally live in deeper water than largemouths, where light levels are usually lower, and they are therefore not quite so adversely affected by cold fronts.

11. If you've been fishing a mid-lake or tailwater section of a body of water, where the water is clear, and suddenly find yourself faced with a cold front, explore the headwater section of the lake where there is sure to be colored water. There, bass behavior is not so adversely affected by the dazzling bright light that typically shocks fish when the trailing edge of the front arrives.

12. If you've planned to fish a local lake or reservoir, and a cold front suddenly moves into your region, consider fishing a river

If a cold front causes bass activity to shut down at your local lake, try switching to a stream or river where bass are unaffected by frontal conditions because of the current.

instead. Because all rivers have a current, they always have more particulate matter in suspension, and hence greater color. In fact, bass of all species that live in large rivers are often unaffected by cold fronts.

13. Bass behavior may be broken down into three components: active, negative, and neutral. Active behavior means the fish are purposely feeding and will aggressively take lures or live baits. Negative behavior means the fish are not purposely feeding and will ignore even the most enticing prey item. Neutral behavior means that bass are not purposely feeding, but that reflex strike responses can be elicited from them if a food item is presented right in front of them. The behavior of bass under cold front conditions is somewhere between neutral and negative.

14. To catch bass under cold front conditions in deep natural lakes and impoundments, fish much deeper than you normally would at that particular time of year. Now is the time to downgrade to lighter testing lines and smaller lures. Better still, switch to live

Bass Activity Modes

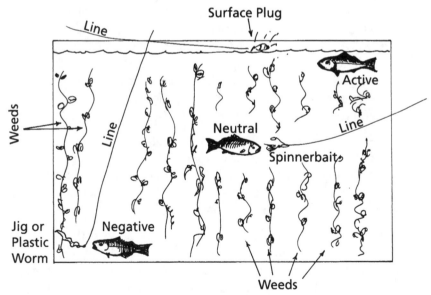

Bass activity levels are described as active, neutral, and negative. Depending upon their behavior mode, the correct lure choice can vary widely.

baits as they can be worked in stationary positions for long periods of time.

15. In shallow natural lakes and reservoirs, focus on the thickest weeds you can find. The best are species such as hydrilla and milfoil, which commonly blanket large surface areas. Look for tiny holes and pockets in the vegetation, quietly ease in close and, using heavier-than-usual line, flip a weedless jig or Texas-rigged plastic worm into the opening and allow it to sink all the way to the bottom. Dress the jig with a pork frog or live minnow to make it even more enticing.

16. In explaining their lack of fishing success, bass anglers often blame "the dog days of summer" and the unusually warm water temperatures sometimes encountered. In actuality, from spring on, a bass' body metabolism steadily increases as the water temperature rises. By the time midsummer arrives, bass are more active than at any other time of year, with a food intake that may be 20 times more than that of winter. Biologists say that 82°F is the temperature at which bass activity peaks; if the water temperature climbs higher than that, bass reverse direction and become less and less active.

17. Generally, only flatland reservoirs, eutrophic natural lakes, and small farm ponds are likely to see midsummer water temperatures rise above 82°F, and then only in their most shallow sections. The solution is to simply move toward the deeper sections, where bass activity levels are sure to be more normal. An option is to move to a mesotrophic natural lake, highland reservoir, or canyonland reservoir.

18. If the only local body of water you regularly fish is very shallow and prone to excessively warm water temperatures in summer, check your map to see if any natural springs or sinkholes are present; both will have cooler water than surrounding areas. Also try fishing shadier parts of the lake.

19. In the face of unusually high water temperatures, think shade. The water temperature beneath a widespread, heavily matted weedbed may be as much as 12°F cooler than its perimeter edges, which border open water. The temperature beneath large docks and piers may be as much as 5°F cooler.

20. Barometric pressure affects bass activity by influencing the fish's use of its swim bladder to maintain its position with a minimal

When the summer water temperature rises to high levels in a shallow lake, cast your lures into shady areas such as underneath docks and shoreline trees with outspread branches. Also try fishing thickly matted weedbeds.

expenditure of energy. A low barometric pressure makes it difficult for bass to remain at mid-depths. As a result, the fish have a tendency to sink to the bottom and go into a negative behavioral mode. A high barometric pressure allows a bass to maintain any depth it chooses with barely having to move a fin.

21. As a rule, a slowly rising barometer provides the best fishing action. A sudden, fast-falling barometer may also provide good fishing, as this condition occurs just prior to the arrival of a storm front. However, a very low barometer that remains low for days at a time, or a very high barometer that remains high for days at a time, usually turns off the fishing action.

22. Wind is a phenomenon that many anglers don't use to their advantage. If the wind is gusting mildly and there is a choppy surface, most anglers fish protected bays, creek arms, and shorelines on the lee side of the lake, where calm water makes boat control and casting lures easier. But the bass there are seldom

as active as those on the windward side of the lake. On the windward side, schools of baitfish are unable to maintain their equilibrium. As the schools become disjointed, with individual fish catapulted one way and then another, bass move in to gorge upon the forage's vulnerability. The same fate awaits crayfish that are dislodged from hiding places as weather-created water currents agitate the bottom mire and sweep across gravel shoals and rocky shorelines. So long as you can do it safely, fish the exposed eastern, northeastern, and southeastern sections of a lake during windy weather.

23. If the prevailing wind direction is flowing parallel to a shoreline, some of the hottest fishing action can occur along shoreline points. When the wind speed is moderate, it creates current that sweeps baitfish down the lengths of shorelines to bass waiting in ambush on the upwind sides of these points.

24. If the wind speed is gusting strongly, bass will have difficulty maintaining their positions on the upwind sides of points and will relocate to the downwind sides. The current will push the

When the wind is gusting, many anglers head for protected coves and creek arms on the lee side of the lake. But, if safety allows for it, the windward side is likely to see bass far more active.

baitfish against the upwind side of the point and then around the tip of the point, allowing bass to dart out from their quiet holding locations to grab the prey.

25. All living creatures possess internal biological clocks that govern behavior. These timing mechanisms operate involuntarily due to a combination of forces that affect every living creature. Scientists have discovered that the activity levels of various organisms can be charted in calendar form with a fair degree of accuracy. Bass anglers in particular are fans of these calendars, hoping to be on the water during the peak activity levels of the fish.

26. The most popular of these calendars are the *Solunar Tables,* formulated by John Alden Knight and first described in his book *Moon Up, Moon Down* (1934). Translating this homespun aphorism into more scientific terminology, *up* refers to when the moon crosses the meridian of longitude overhead, *down* to when it crosses the meridian on its return trip underneath the planet. During these times, the combined effects of solar (sun) and lunar (moon) gravitational pull exerts its greatest force upon our planet. Ocean tidal activity is the most obvious result. But Knight's research also indicates heightened activity in every living creature from the lowest insect forms to *homo sapiens.*

27. Since the moon day is nearly one hour longer than our 24-hour earth day, the *Solunar Tables* have a so-called lag time in which each day's peak activity periods for bass occur one hour later than the day before. *Solunar Tables* are currently published each month in more than 60 newspapers nationwide and in numerous sportsmen's magazines.

28. Since the introduction of the *Solunar Tables,* many other creature-activity calendars have evolved. The basis for all of them is the gravitational pull of the sun and moon, but various researchers have also incorporated into their predictions variations for standard or daylight saving time, sunrise and sunset schedules, daily fishing logs from full-time guides, data from record-keeping agencies, and other information.

29. Florida bass researcher Doug Hannon produces a calendar known as the *Moon Clock,* available in many tackleshops and mail-order fishing catalogs. His most startling finding, which includes all fish

Bass have internal biological clocks that govern their levels of activity. Many believe the gravitational effects of the moon regulate their behavior.

There are many types of tables that reveal specific times of day when bass will display activity-level highs and lows.

species, is that 41 percent of the world records were caught within the period of two days before a full moon to two days after.

30. All of the researchers who have produced activity calendars admit there is one flaw in their predictions: Such calendars are reasonably accurate only during stable weather and water conditions. During periods of instability, bass are their usual unpredictable selves. The reader may wish to regularly consult one of these calendars so that, if his scheduling allows for it, he can be on the water during predicted activity periods. But the angler should know that a major cold front, a sudden fluctuation in barometric pressure, a pool-level drawdown by a lake's managing agency, or other local conditions may override any calendar predictions.

To determine which fish-activity calendars are most accurate, and what fishing techniques work best under various weather conditions, many serious bass anglers keep logbooks and refer to them often.

43 Tackle Tips on Selecting Rods, Reels, and Lines

Your equipment determines your ability to effectively present lures and baits to bass—and to catch them.

The best tackle is expensive, but it does pay off in trouble-free performance, is a pleasure to use, and will allow you to hook and land far more bass.

1. Always purchase the best tackle you can afford. It will last much longer than cheaper merchandise, it will be a joy to use, and it will reward you with more and bigger bass.

2. The spincasting reel—also known as the closed-faced or push-button reel—is the only type not recommended for serious bass anglers. Its trouble-free design and ease of use are suitable for introducing youngsters to fishing, but virtually no full-time guides

or professionals on the tournament circuit use them. Why? Because they're inexpensive, they are not made from finely machined parts, they are not rugged or designed for hard use, and they do not have smooth-running drags.

3. Manufacturers of the highest-quality open-face spinning and baitcasting reels include Abu-Garcia, Daiwa, Fin-Nor, Mitchell, Penn, Quantum, Shakespeare, and Shimano.

4. Each reel manufacturer has three grades: economy, intermediate, and professional. I wouldn't recommend acquiring a reel of less than "intermediate" grade.

5. Reading about a reel's components will let you quickly distinguish between a superior model and one that will yield disappointing performance. The best reels are made of machined aircraft aluminum for tight tolerances and have stainless-steel ball bearings to hold internal parts in precise alignment for the smoothest possible operation. Inferior reels are made of stock aluminum and have steel bearings, aluminum bearings, or none at all. Spacers (washers) between other moving components

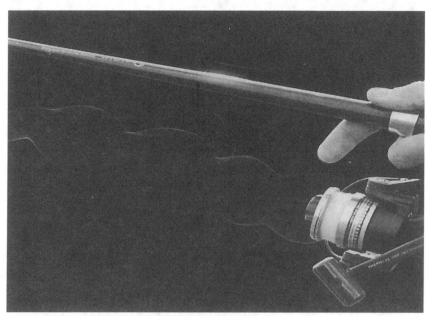

Open-face spinning reels of high quality are made of machined aircraft aluminum and have stainless-steel ball bearings for smooth operation.

(such as the drag mechanism) should be made of graphite or Teflon to reduce friction; inferior reels have plastic spacers.

6. Always select an open-face spinning or baitcasting reel that has a minimum 4.5:1 gear ratio or higher. The gear ratio determines how much line is wound onto the spool with each turn of the handle. For bass fishing, a high gear ratio is desirable for working lures designed to be retrieved at relatively fast speeds, such as buzzbaits and crankbaits. A high gear ratio also lets an angler quickly take up the slack line that sometimes occurs when fishing soft plastic lures; plus it allows him to quickly muscle a bass out and away from thick cover.

7. A desirable feature on baitcasting reels is a centrifugal cast-control knob that may be adjusted to accommodate different lure weights. This allows the angler to gain maximum casting distance with even the lightest lures, while virtually eliminating backlashes.

8. Quality spinning and casting rods are made by All Star, Daiwa, Fenwick, G. Loomis, Shakespeare, Shimano, South Bend, and St. Croix. As with reels, each company offers rods in economy, intermediate, and professional grades. I recommend acquiring rods that are at least of the intermediate level.

9. Several manufacturers offer rods made of fiberglass or fiberglass-composite materials. These are economy-grade rods that serious bass anglers are usually disappointed with.

10. The majority of today's highest-quality rods designed for bass fishing are made of graphite (more properly, high-modulus graphite, or simply HMG). This material is produced by taking a synthetic fiber called polyacrylontrile and heating it to 2500°F to char it. The charred material is then imbedded in a special resin, wrapped around a mandrel (a stainless-steel dummy rod), and baked. When the mandrel is removed, what's left is the graphite rod blank, which is then sanded, lacquered, and outfitted with guides and a combination handle/reel seat.

11. Features that make graphite rods popular with serious bass anglers are that they are lightweight, of very small diameter, and have a very stiff action. The stiff action allows for a fast recovery on the cast. In other words, when the rod is flexed during the cast, it quickly snaps back to its original shape. This means you can make a long cast with a relatively flat trajectory, instead

One of the most desirable features of a baitcasting reel is a cast-control knob that can be adjusted for different lure weights. The highest quality spinning and baitcasting rods are made of high-modulus graphite.

of having a big arc in the line, which is typical when casting with a more limber fiberglass rod with its characteristic slow recovery. As a result, casting accuracy is much better with graphite rods, especially when a strong wind is blowing and one is target fishing by casting spinnerbaits and crankbaits to stumps, standing timber, and weedlines.

12. Another desirable feature of graphite rods is extreme sensitivity in telegraphing information from the rod tip to the handle. In one independent laboratory test, engineers attached transducers (similar to those used with sonar units) to both graphite and fiberglass rods, shot the rod tips with impulses, and then measured their characteristics. They learned that when an impulse was introduced to the tip of a graphite rod, it traveled to the rod handle 120 percent faster than in a conventional fiberglass rod of identical length. This proves that graphite rods are indeed superior tools when fishing soft plastic lures and jigs, in which case there seldom is a solid strike but rather a barely perceptible bump or tap.

13. The most suitable graphite rods designed for bass fishing are those in lengths ranging from six- to seven-and-a-half feet. Anything shorter than six feet is inefficient in terms of casting and hook-setting ability. And anything longer than seven-and-a-half feet undoubtedly will be a two-piece affair that is unwieldy to cast and has a weak spot, midway along the rod's length, in the form of a ferrule connecting the two sections.

14. Most quality spinning and baitcasting rods have an imprint (or label) somewhere on the butt end of the rod blank that provides the angler with information in making the right rod selection for his needs. Such labels show the recommended range of line and lure weights that offer optimum performance with that particular rod. The rod's action will also be described; one manufacturer may use the designations "fast," "mod.fast," or "ex.fast," while another may describe its rod actions as "medium-light," "medium," "medium-heavy," or "heavy." Just keep in mind that when fishing jigs, jigging spoons, or soft plastic lures, you'll want a stiffer rod action to detect the delicate bites than when pitching crankbaits, spinnerbaits, or topwater lures.

15. A spinning or baitcasting rod's guides are extremely important because the material in the guide inserts determines the amount of friction exerted upon the line as it passes through them.

Excessive friction by cheap guide inserts reduces casting distance and inflicts a great amount of wear upon the line. The guides on the highest quality rods are invariably made of some type of hard, polished material such as stainless steel, ceramic, aluminum oxide, tungsten carbide, or titanium.

16. The design and type of material comprising a bass rod's handle may be a molded pistol-grip affair or a straight two-handed handle. The choice involves a good deal of personal preference, but there are a few utilitarian considerations. A pistol-grip handle, usually made of a molded rubber-composite material, may become slippery to hold when wet, whereas a handle made of cork, or compressed closed-cell foam, usually affords a more secure grip. Also, a "shorty" pistol-grip handle doesn't allow for as much leverage in horsing a big fish out of heavy cover as does a two-handed handle that can be braced against the forearm.

17. The reel seat is likewise mostly a matter of personal preference. Most are made of aluminum or graphite, but be sure it has a knurled locking ring that can be tightened down to keep the reel feet from wiggling and eventually working loose.

18. Flyrodding for bass is a laid-back way to enjoy a day on the water. Quality rods are made by Cortland, Fenwick, G. Loomis, Pflueger, Reddington, Scientific Anglers, St. Croix, and White River. Graphite rod blanks and cork handles are by far the most popular with serious anglers. For maximum overall line control, casting accuracy, and distance, a nine-foot (two-piece) rod is recommended. A moderate action allows the rod to load and unload the most efficiently when throwing wind-resistant lures such as poppers, deerhair bugs, and oversized streamers.

19. Due to the large-diameter, abrasion-resistant lines that are typically used with fly rods, the hard chrome or stainless-steel snake guides on most flyrods are adequate. However, be sure the larger stripper guide (the guide closest to the reel) has a ceramic insert. Also be sure the rod has an aluminum reel seat with a locking ring; some flyrods have only two non-locking rings on the cork handle that slip over the reel feet.

20. Quality fly reels are made by the same manufacturers of spinning and baitcasting reels. There are two types: so-called "automatic" models and single-action reels. With the auto reel, each

A high-quality spinning or baitcasting rod will have guides made of high-tech metals or ceramics, but even they can become damaged. Use a Q-Tip to check for cracks or rough surfaces that can nick or fray the line.

Pistol-grip handles on baitcasting rods are the best sellers, but more and more anglers are switching to straight-handled rods that afford greater leverage in horsing bass out of heavy cover.

time the angler strips out line, a coiled spring inside the reel housing is loaded; by pressing a lever, the angler releases the spring, which uncoils and retrieves line back onto the reel arbor until the lever is released. A single-action reel is manually operated. In either case, a Size 2 reel mates perfectly with the nine-foot rod mentioned above.

With fly rods, you cast the line, not the fly; it simply goes along for the ride. The best all-round flyrod length is nine feet.

21. Unlike spinning and baitcasting reels, it's not necessary to be overly concerned about high-quality materials and construction in a fly reel intended for bass fishing. Fly reels play no role in casting lures and little role in fighting modestly sized fish; for the most part, they are simply line-storage devices. However, since it is not uncommon to catch bass over five pounds on fly tackle, you should select an intermediate-grade reel that has an internal drag disk made of Teflon or graphite.

22. The two leading manufacturers of quality fly lines are Cortland and Scientific Anglers. Unlike monofilament lines that have various pound-test ratings, fly lines are rated by weight, with an 8-weight line being the best choice to go with the nine-foot rod and Size 2 reel mentioned earlier.

23. Fly lines come in level and tapered, as well as floating and sinking, varieties. Tapered lines are intended only for lightweight flies. For heavy casting poppers and deerhair bugs, use the floating no-taper (level) type. If you were to try to use a tapered line, it would not turn over on the cast to deliver the heavy popper or bug but would simply fall in a heap on the water.

24. When fishing streamers in shallow water (less than four feet deep), use a floating fly line with a sinking tip. In water deeper than four feet, use a sinking fly line.

25. You'll need to attach a leader to the terminal end of the fly line, and your lure to the other end of the leader. When casting poppers and bugs, most anglers simply use an eight-foot length of standard monofilament in 8- to 12-pound test.

26. When casting oversized streamers, the same eight-foot mono leader in 8- to 12-pound test is suitable. When using small streamers, however, a tapered leader such as 3× (6-pound test) is recommended.

27. When buying a fly reel, many anglers like to get an extra, interchangeable spool. This way, if you intend to fish both heavy and lightweight lures on a given outing (say, surface bugs in the morning and sinking streamers in the afternoon), it's easy to snap out one spool containing one type of line and replace it with another.

28. When flyrodding from the bow of a bass boat, drape a towel over the electric motor's control cables lying on the front decking. This won't hamper the motor's operation, but will minimize fly-line tangles.

When flyrodding from the bow of a boat that's outfitted with an electric motor and sonar device, drape a towel over the equipment to prevent flyline tangles when casting.

43 Tackle Tips on Selecting Rods, Reels, and Lines　　　**175**

29. Quality monofilament lines for use with spinning and bait-casting reels are manufactured by Abu Garcia, Berkley, Excaliber, Maxima, Silver Thread, SpiderWire, and Stren. Although the weights of lines from these companies range from 2- to 50-pound test, the weights most commonly used for bass fishing with spinning reels ranges from 6- to 17-pound test; with baitcasting reels, the range is generally from 12- to 30-pound test.

30. In addition to a wide range of pound tests, most manufacturers also make mono lines in various degrees of abrasion resistance. The "softest" lines (least abrasion-resistant) offer the smoothest casting, greatest distance, and best accuracy. Their drawback is that they can quickly break upon coming in contact with the sharp, angular edges of underwater rocks and coarse brush and tree bark. Because of this, it's generally best to use soft lines only in lake regions that have little cover.

31. So-called "hard lines" (the most abrasion resistant) allow an angler to work lures in and around the thickest cover imaginable, and to horse big bass out of brushpiles and submerged tree

Abrasion-resistant lines are ideal for working lures through brittle cover such as brush and tree branches. They can be unmanageable in cold weather, however.

crowns. The downside of hard lines is that they can be a bit stiff and wiry, especially in cold weather, and this impedes smooth casting, distance, and accuracy.

32. Many anglers like to have several rigged rods in their boats at any given time. This gives them the opportunity to switch lures in an instant, simply by picking up another rod. Typically, each rod has a different lure and line with differing abrasion resistance. If one rod/reel combo is set up to fish a plastic worm or jig in heavy brush cover, the reel will be loaded with a highly abrasion-resistant "hard" line. Another rod/reel combo set up for fishing a spinnerbait through grass beds may have a moderately abrasion-resistant line. And a rod/reel outfit set up for fishing a crankbait along sheer, smooth, underwater rock walls may have a soft line.

33. Monofilament lines are available in a rainbow of colors. Choosing one may seem perplexing, but there are a few simple guidelines to keep in mind. When fishing spinnerbaits and crankbaits, for example, try to match the line color to the water color, so the line is less visible to bass.

34. Use an optically brightened line that appears to "glow" when you're fishing soft plastic baits and jigs. With these lures, you're more likely to see the strike rather than feel it. The line will twitch or jump, and you want to be able to see it. While this line may be visible above the surface, its fluorescence is not so obvious underwater.

35. Dr. Fred Janzow, a fishery biologist at Missouri State University, studied hundreds of bass in laboratory test tanks and noted their reactions to lines of different colors. He found, for instance, that bass exhibited alarm responses and were repelled by lures tied to bright yellow lines. Lures with lines of subtle hues (light blue, pale green, and clear) yielded the most favorable responses.

36. There's no need for a bass angler to learn the countless types of knots that have been conceived over the years, as two styles— the Palomar knot and the improved clinch knot—will suit almost every need and circumstance. The Palomar knot is recommended for soft plastic lures, in which the hook's line-tie and associated knot are buried inside the head. The improved clinch knot is favored for most other lures.

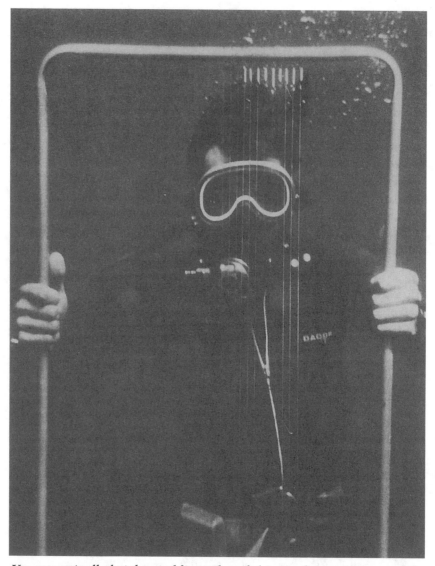

Use an optically brightened line when fishing soft plastic lures and jigs so you can see bites that you can't feel through the rod tip. Biologists say light blue, pale green, and clear-colored lines are the least alarming to bass.

37. Using an Instron Tensile Strength Testing Machine, scientists at Stren, the largest mono line manufacturer, found that there is no scientific evidence that spitting on a knot while drawing it up tight is beneficial to the connection's strength. Knots

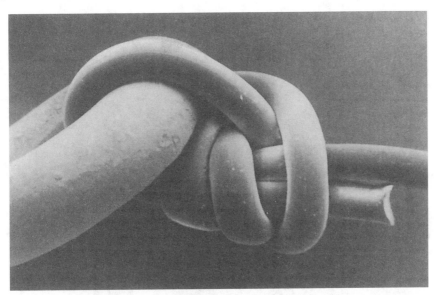

Use the Palomar knot when fishing soft plastic lures, in which the hook's line-tie and knot are buried inside the head.

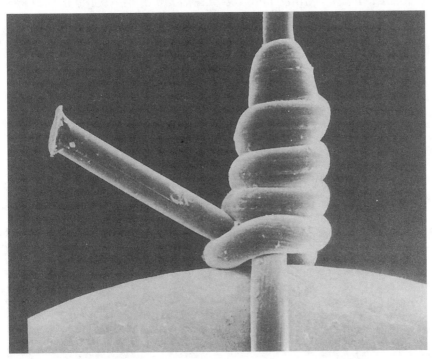

Use the improved clinch knot for plugs, spoons, spinnerbaits, buzzbaits, jigs, and flyrod lures.

43 Tackle Tips on Selecting Rods, Reels, and Lines   **179**

The drag mechanisms on spinning and baitcasting reels must be adjusted in accordance with the pound test of line being used. On a spinning reel, the drag is a dial on the front of the line spool or a knob at the rear of the reel housing.

Use a small hand scale to help you set the drag.

tied with both wet and dry lines proved to be equal in strength.

38. When putting new line onto a spinning reel, fill the spool only to within one-eighth inch of the flange. With a baitcasting reel, fill the spool only to within one-quarter inch of the flange. Over-filling a reel can cause line tangles and backlashes, while under-filling it retards casting distance and accuracy.

39. Once line has been spooled onto a reel, be sure to adjust the drag mechanism. Usually comprised of a series of layered washers, the drag is designed to slip and release line at a lower force than that required to break the line. The generally accepted figure is to set the drag at no more than 25 percent of the line's rated breaking strength. If you're using 20-pound-test line, for example, the drag should be set to yield when five pounds of pressure is exerted upon it. A small hand scale will help you set the drag at the correct amount of pressure.

40. Once a reel's drag is set, tie the terminal end of the line to an immovable object, back off the length of a cast, and then put a good bend in your rod until the drag begins slipping. Does the drag release line smoothly? Or does the rod tip bounce erratically as line is being released? If the latter is the case, the same "stuttering" will occur when you hook a big fish, and you'll probably lose him. To correct the problem, dissemble and clean the reel, as dirt and grit have probably accumulated inside the drag.

41. If your mono line becomes twisted, your casting accuracy and distance will become greatly impaired. This occurs far more fre-quently with spinning reels than with baitcasters. The solution is to clip off your lure and allow about 40 yards of the bare line to trail out behind your boat under slow trolling speed. The cavitation of the outboard's lower unit will straighten the line in just a few minutes.

42. When fishing, periodically run your fingertips over the terminal three feet of your line. If you detect nicks, cuts, or rough places, do not hesitate to cut back the end of the line and tie a new knot. When fishing soft plastic lures and jigs in tree tops and heavy brush, many anglers check the terminal ends of the lines every few minutes throughout the day.

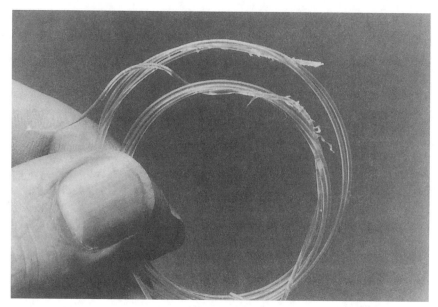

Especially when fishing in brushy cover or brittle weeds, regularly check the terminal end of your line. Cut it back several feet if you feel nicks or abrasion. Dispose of it properly.

43. Always store extra spools of line in their original packaging in an area that is cool and not exposed to light.

35 Ways to Fish Live Baits

Sometimes, nothing works like the real thing.

Live baits are deadly on bass day or night, hot or cold.

1. Live baits have many advantages. They have the appearance, movements, smell, taste, and texture of the prey that bass are accustomed to eating on a daily basis. This means that when weather or water conditions have thrown bass into a neutral or negative state of activity, and they're not aggressively striking at artificial lures, live baits may save the day.

2. Even when bass are active, they don't engage in "chase and catch" feeding behavior if the water temperature is below 55°F. Consider fishing live baits as such times, as they can be presented at much slower speeds than most artificial lures.

3. Live baits do have their disadvantages. They are somewhat messy to handle and, since they are living creatures, you need to have a good livewell or some other method of keeping them alive and healthy. Since live baits are generally fished very slowly, it can also take an angler much longer to find bass locations with bait than with search-and-find artificial lures, which cover much larger expanses of water in shorter time frames.

4. Bass are opportunistic feeders and will forage upon a wide range of prey species, some of them more or less abundant in particular waters or at certain times of year. These prey species

may include frogs, tadpoles and other amphibians, eels, small snakes, aquatic and terrestrial insects, and even birds and mice upon occasion. But tops on their list of preferred items are crayfish and smaller fish, including baitfish species such as threadfin and gizzard shad, golden and emerald shiners, and fathead and bluntnose minnows. In northern waters, they may also feed upon baitfish species such as smelt, herring, alewives, ciscoes, and young panfish or other gamefish.

5. When deciding which live baits to use, inquire at bait stores near the lake or river you intend to fish. They'll know what the predominant forage base is in that water, and most likely will have it on hand. The only bait that state laws prohibit anglers from using are young gamefish. If a bait dealer says he has "bass minnows" in stock, they're not really fingerling bass; they're undoubtedly three-inch fathead or bluntnose minnows or one of the shiner species.

6. Fisheries biologists who study bass behavior in laboratory tanks say that all three bass species go through a ritual before they start looking for food. The first behavior is called a "gaping reflex," in which the bass appears to be yawning. Biologists liken this to a jogger who stretches before running, only with a bass it is to quicken its reflexes. Bass also commonly erect their dorsal fins prior to feeding, but no one knows why.

7. Curiously, bass and their prey often hover side by side without incident, occasionally even brushing against each other with swimming tails and fins. The instant any bass begins "yawning," however, or erects its dorsal spines, every potential prey in the vicinity goes on full alert. Some make mad dashes for the safety of cover, while others freeze in position. Then, in less time than it takes to read this sentence, some biological mechanism triggers the bass's feeding desire and the nearest minnow disappears.

8. When a bass engulfs a food item, it quickly opens its mouth while simultaneously flaring its gill covers and expelling water through the gills. This creates a suction effect, allowing the bass to inhale its prey. By the same token, a bass can expel a food item (or a lure) just as quickly, simply by reversing the suction process and blowing the food from its mouth. This briefly brings us back to the strong endorsement for high-quality graphite rods discussed in the last chapter. Because of their sensitivity,

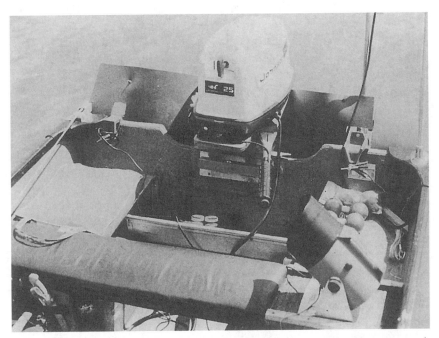

The most popular and effective method of presenting live baits is with the technique known as backtrolling. On this boat, perfectly outfitted for backtrolling, note the splashguard behind the outboard; since the boat is operated in reverse, the guard prevents water from coming over the transom in choppy surface conditions.

graphite rods are ideal for detecting delicate bites or anything else that's happening at the terminal end of the line. Always heed the adage, "If in doubt, strike!"

9. The most effective method of presenting a wide range of live baits to bass is the one conceived by Bill Binkelman of Milwaukee, Wisconsin, and later by Al and Ron Lindner of Brainerd, Minnesota. Known variously as *backtrolling, Lindy-rigging* or simply, *rigging,* this technique employs various species of minnows or shiners, and nightcrawlers. In some regions, such as the northern border states, leeches and crayfish are frequently used. Elsewhere, particularly in the South and Midwest, salamanders are popular; depending upon the region, salamanders may be referred to as spring lizards, mud puppies, waterdogs, sirens, or sallies.

10. The required tackle for backtrolling is a medium-action spinning rod with an open-face spinning reel loaded with 8-to

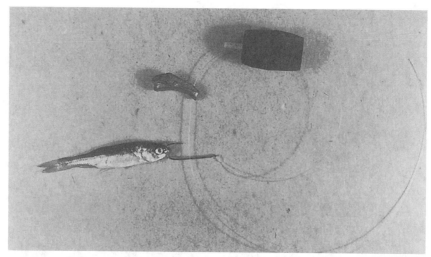

When rigging to backtroll live baits, first thread the line through a shoe-shaped sinker before tying it to a hook. If the bottom is muddy or silty, add a small foam bobber to keep the bait a foot or more above the bottom.

10-pound monofilament. Most anglers use a conventional aluminum V-bottom boat with a tiller-controlled outboard, although the technique can also be used with a bow-mounted electric motor.

11. The "rigging" aspect of backtrolling involves threading the terminal end of the line through a special sliding sinker; those shaped like a shoe are best because of their ability to ride over rocks and other bottom obstructions with a minimal chance of snagging. The average size of the sinker is one-quarter ounce, but this can change depending on water depth, current, or wind. Pass the line through the hole in the sinker, then tie on a small swivel. Next tie one end of a four-foot length of monofilament to the swivel's other eyelet, and attach a Size 8, long-shanked Aberdeen hook to the terminal end of the line. The swivel prevents the sinker from sliding all the way down the "leader" to the hook, while the hole in the slip-sinker allows the line to travel unimpeded whenever you want it to. This system lets you present your live bait right on the bottom at any depth and at speeds ranging from very slow to dead stop. No casting is involved.

12. When backtrolling a lake area where the bottom is comprised of a thick layer of mire, dragging a live bait through that silt and

For backtrolling, always hook leeches and 'crawlers through the tip of the nose.

mud hides it from view. In this situation, many anglers like to attach a small foam bobber to the line, two feet above the bait. The sinker will continue to remain on the bottom, but the bobber will float upward and thus keep the bait suspended slightly above the bottom.

13. In rigging, hook a nightcrawler through the dark tip of the nose (the light-colored flat end is the tail); hook a minnow through both lips; hook a leech through the sucker disk; and hook a crayfish through the tail. Salamanders should never be hooked through the lips because they must be able to open and close their mouths to work their gills; instead, run the hook through the nostrils.

14. In backtrolling, and presenting the bait to bass, begin by opening the bail of your spinning reel and allowing line to pay out until you feel the sliding sinker hit bottom. Do *not* turn the reel handle to close the bail. Instead, curl your index finger around the slack line and hold it lightly. The boat's outboard or electric motor can now be used to slowly maneuver you around as the lure is dragged across the bottom, along breaklines and over various other features where you might expect to find bass.

Backtrolling presents the slowly-swimming bait directly beneath the boat. Spinning tackle is recommended, with the reel's bail open and the line curled around the index finger. At the first indication of a strike, release the line. After the bass takes the bait, close the bail and strike.

Most anglers use the outboard or electric motor in reverse gear, so the boat's broad transom pushes into the current, thus achieving the slowest possible momentum.

15. With your eye on a sonar screen, as you try different depths, it will periodically be necessary to take in or let out a bit of slack line, but for all practical purposes you'll be fishing almost directly beneath the boat at all times. Do not allow a long line to pay out far behind the boat, as you would when trolling artificial lures.

16. In backtrolling, a "bite" may take many forms, depending on the water temperature and the activity level of the bass. Sometimes you won't feel anything, but will suddenly see your line jump. Other times there will be an obvious bump feeling. Still other times there may be a strange sensation of nothing on the end of your line, as though the terminal rigging was cut off; this indicates that a bass has picked up your bait and is swimming toward you with it. Other times there may be a steady resis-

tance at the end of the line, as if you've picked up a ball of weeds.

17. In backtrolling, determining when to strike requires a bit of trial and error. Most anglers begin the day by hitting them quickly. When you sense a bass has taken the bait, immediately release the line curled around your finger, lower the rod tip, engage the reel's bail, take up any slack, and strike, all in an instant. If you miss several fish this way, give the next one a five-count before striking; then, if you miss, try a 10-count on the next one. As a rule, the colder the water, the longer you have to let the bass mouth the bait before he entirely takes it in and the hook is in position for striking.

18. When prey species are injured, they emit distress vibrations which nearby bass can easily detect. As a result, some anglers like to clip a minnow's tail or break off one of a crayfish's claws, to make these two live baits more effective.

19. To keep minnows and salamanders fresh and frisky, use un-chlorinated, heavily aerated water in whatever container you're using. If they begin coming to the surface to gulp air, they're in trouble. Many minnow buckets have small, internal, battery-operated aerators. A boat with an aerated livewell can also be used.

20. Nightcrawlers and crayfish must be kept very cool; heat will quickly kill them. A plastic-foam bait box with a tight-fitting lid and containing damp sphagnum peat moss or worm bedding is best. If you're on the water for a long time, periodically add a few ice cubes from your beverage cooler.

21. Leeches require ice cold, unchlorinated water. They're commonly stored in plastic containers with ice cubes. Be sure the lid fits tightly, as leeches like to travel. Leeches may attach themselves to your fingers during handling, but they're harmless. Simply pull them off.

22. In all forms of live-bait fishing, bass typically have the oppor-tunity to inspect an angler's offering before deciding whether to take it. Any unnatural odor on the bait will cause bass to reject it. So whenever you fill your outboard's gas tank, handle your trolling motor battery, or do anything else in which a foreign substance or odor may be transferred to your hands, be sure to wash them with an odor-eliminating sportsman's soap.

Onboard storage of live bait is critical to success. The bait must be kept cool, fresh and frisky. Many anglers use large containers for storing live baits in an old refrigerator, and transfer them to smaller containers for each day's fishing.

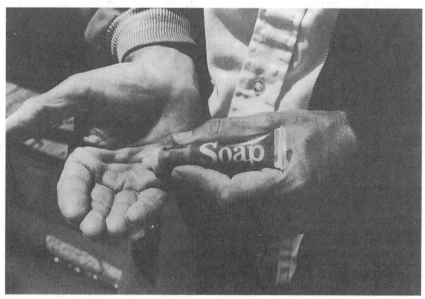

Never allow noxious odors to be transferred to your baits. Wash your hands with an odor-eliminating soap after fueling your outboard tank, handling trolling motor batteries, or eating your lunch.

23. Sallies afford exciting action because they commonly eat newly hatched bass fry and destroy spawning beds. Because of this, bass will try to kill them at every opportunity, whether they're hungry or not. Sallies look rather intimidating, but don't be afraid to handle them because they don't bite, and none of the North American species are poisonous.

24. Salamanders are very hardy, so it's often possible to catch many bass on a single bait before having to replace it. Repeated casting will quickly kill a salamander, however, which is why many anglers prefer to backtroll them.

25. Another way to fish a salamander is to hook it through the nostrils and use no sinker on the line. Simply lower the sally into the water and it will immediately begin swimming to the bottom, toward the nearest cover. The best place to do this is near the edge of a thick weedbed that mats the surface, wherever there are jumbled rock piles on the bottom, or in the vicinity of logs and tree crowns on the lake floor.

26. With its four moving legs and tail whipping from side to side for propulsion, a sally can swim very quickly. Because they like to

Salamanders provide exciting fishing because bass aggressively try to kill them before taking them into their mouths. Sallies are very hardy; you can catch many bass on each one.

head for cover, periodically raise your rod tip and pull the sally back a few feet, to keep it exposed and moving on the bottom.

27. When a bass attacks a salamander, the experience is unmistakable, as your line will begin strumming like a banjo string. Don't strike yet! The bass is trying to kill the salamander and has not yet fully taken the bait into its mouth. Wait until you see the line beginning to move away before reeling in any slack and attempting to set the hook.

28. A unique form of live-bait fishing in the deep South is shiner fishing for the Florida-strain largemouth. The goal is to take bass that weigh 10 pounds or more. In tempting such big fish, the baits must also be oversize. Most anglers prefer golden shiners, which run six to eight inches in length, and which may cost $1 or more apiece.

29. Shiner fishing for big bass is almost always done on relatively shallow flatland reservoirs or natural eutrophic lakes, where the average water depth is no more than 15 feet and there are wide expanses of heavily matted weeds ringing the shoreline. The mid-lake areas are also thick with weeds layering the bottom, but they grow up to only within several feet of the surface and are pockmarked with holes and channels.

30. Although heavy-duty spinning tackle can be used, most "trophy hunters" opt for a baitcasting reel on a stout, long-handled rod. The line should be 25- to 30-pound-test abrasion-resistant monofilament. The terminal tackle commonly consists of a 4/0 or 5/0 hook and just barely enough weight on the line to prevent the shiner from swimming to the surface.

31. Two types of shiner fishing are the most popular. The first sees the angler beginning on the lee side of the lake and making repeated drifts across the open, mid-lake areas with the wind. Shiners are hooked through both lips and suspended beneath large bobbers so they are permitted to "swim" just above the weed tops. After one pass is made, the angler motors back to the opposite side of the lake and makes another drift, this time from a slightly different starting point so he covers new water. The bass lie deep in the weeds, often in a hole or in association with some type of bottom configuration, and periodically rise to pick off baitfish passing overhead. When the bobber ducks under, or begins moving away, the angler gives the bass a few seconds to inhale the bait before attempting to set the hook.

Shiner fishing for the giant Florida bass subspecies can produce explosive action. It's usually restricted to shallow flatland reservoirs and natural eutrophic lakes.

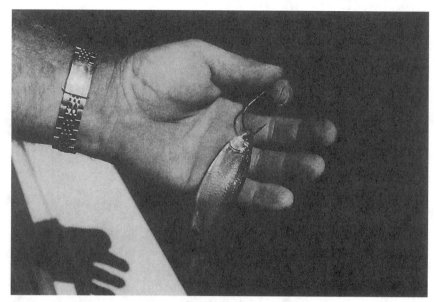

Hook six- to 10-inch golden shiners once through the lips. A favored way of fishing them is allowing them to swim far back under matted vegetation where lures cannot be presented.

32. The second method of shiner fishing is done around the matted shoreline weeds; in this case, bass are likely to be far back under the canopy of cover, hiding in dark catacombs where it's impossible to get a lure to them. The same rod, reel, line, and hook are used, but no weight is placed on the line and no bobber is employed. Positioning his boat 20 yards or so from the weedline edge, the angler lowers his shiner over the side and begins paying out line. The shiner instantly heads for the perceived safety of the weeds, often swimming 25 yards or more back under the matted vegetation.

33. When shiner fishing, an angler may receive several different types of strikes. On occasion the line will begin vibrating because the shiner, upon seeing a bass approaching, actually begins trembling. Other times you'll feel a steady resistance or weighty sensation at the end of the line. Still other times, far back in the weeds, you'll see the surface water bulge up or boil, which indicates that a big bass has taken the bait. In all of these cases, don't strike immediately; wait a moment until the bass has the bait fully in its mouth.

A second method of shiner fishing is drifting them over bottom vegetation in mid-lake areas. When you reach the end of the drift, motor back to the opposite side of the weedy area and begin another drift from a new starting point.

34. Live-bait fishing can also be done in streams and mid-sized shallow rivers where the water cascades around rocks and other obstructions that divert the flow. Largemouths will hold in the calm areas behind these obstructions, especially along undercut banks. Smallmouths will be in the faster flowing water. And spotted bass will be associating with cover near the edges of milder current flows.

35. Since bass in streams and small rivers don't grow to large size, light to medium-light spinning tackle is recommended. Lines exceeding 10-pound test are rarely needed. The most commonly used baits include hellgrammites, small crayfish, minnows, and worms. Casting these delicate baits is not recommended because they'll quickly die or tear off the hook. Hook the chosen bait once, lightly, using a Size 6 or 8 hook, and add

a single split-shot to the line. Now simply feed out line incrementally, allowing the bait to slowly tumble downstream with the current. Since bass know that prey coming downstream with the flow will be gone in a second if they don't react instantly, strikes are quick and decisive, so don't hesitate in setting the hook.

38 Methods for Fishing Crankbaits and Topwater Lures

These search lures allow you to find and catch bass quickly.

Crankbaits and topwater lures allow anglers to find bass quickly. They then have the option of thoroughly working the area with slower lures.

1. Crankbaits are a specific breed of plugs made from hollow plastic, balsa, ABS foam and, sometimes, cedar. The one thing they all have in common is that they are designed to be retrieved at moderate to very fast speeds, and in most instances represent fleeing baitfish or panfish.

2. Most crankbaits float at rest, dive to certain depths on the retrieve, and then exhibit a tight wiggling action as they track their way back to the boat. Because of these characteristics, crankbaits are generally used when the water temperature is warm (60°F or higher) and the bass are active. The most popular crankbaits for bass fishing are three to five inches long and weigh one-quarter to three-quarters of an ounce.

3. Each crankbait has its own narrow range of depth, which depends primarily on the width, length, and slant of the plastic bill on the plug's nose. One crankbait may run two to four feet deep, for example, while another with a longer or more acutely angled bill may dive to six to 10 feet. There are currently no crankbaits on the market that run deeper than 20 feet, so in

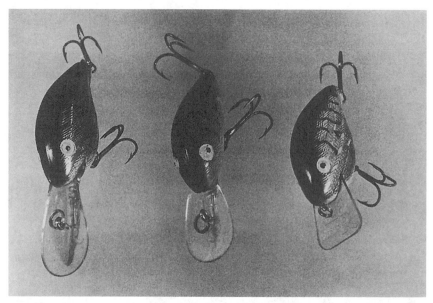

These crankbaits are identical in size and weight, but the different bills on their noses will take them down to different depths on the retrieve.

addition to warm water situations they are typically used for fishing shoreline cover and relatively shallow bottom structures or contours in mid-lake regions.

4. The depth range of a crankbait is usually stated somewhere on the lure's packaging. In addition to the depth range that the manufacturer has built into a given crankbait, the angler can manipulate the depth at which the plug runs by increasing or decreasing retrieval speed.

5. The pound test of the line being used, or its diameter, also influences a crankbait's running depth. An abrasion-resistant, thick-diameter 15-pound-test line will cause a crankbait to run somewhat shallower than an identical crankbait tied to a thin 15-pound-test line.

6. Crankbaits are available in a wide range of body profiles to simulate various species of forage. Bass anglers usually have the most success by using crankbaits that represent the primary forage base in a given body of water. If you're fishing a flatland reservoir where the bass primarily feed upon bluegills, use a "fat plug" that is short, blocky, and has panfish colorations.

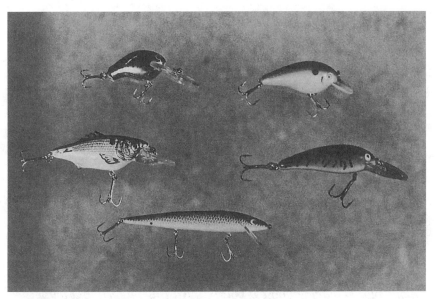

Crankbaits come in a wide range of body profiles. Use whichever matches the forage base in the water you're fishing.

7. If you're fishing a highland reservoir where bass primarily feed upon threadfin shad, use a crankbait that's more elongated and has a representative baitfish color.

8. If you're fishing a natural mesotrophic lake, where the bass primarily feed on shiners, dace, or yellow perch, use a slim-minnow-type crankbait in an appropriate color.

9. A recent survey of tournament anglers revealed six must-have crankbait colors that will give you greatest versatility on almost any body of water. They are shad-gray, mullet-blue, perch, bone, crayfish (brown with orange belly), and bluegill-sunfish (chartreuse with black back).

10. Many brands of crankbaits come in so-called "naturalized" or "photo-imprint" finishes, in which there are detailed eyes, fins, and even scales that make them look very lifelike. There seems to be a consensus among pro anglers that these features are designed more to catch fishermen than fish because, when retrieved at even the slowest speeds, the vibrating, tight-wiggling action of the lure causes such detailed features to "blur out" and become indistinguishable to bass. This is especially the case in colored or muddy water. When fishing in clear water, it's better

As a rule, in clear water use a crankbait with a subdued body pattern. In off-colored water, choose a bold, contrasting pattern that will make the lure more visible.

to stick with pale baitfish colors. In off-colored or muddy water, use gaudy colors and large, boldly contrasting patterns.

11. When preparing to tie on a crankbait in a crayfish pattern, make sure that the one you choose from your tacklebox can go deep enough to dig into the bottom where you're fishing. In so doing, the bill on the nose of the lure will kick up puffs of silt and bottom mire to simulate a real crayfish scurrying around.

12. It's wise to carry at least three crankbaits in each of the colors mentioned in Tip No. 9. This way you'll have spares in case you lose a few. It is just as important to have crankbaits in each color that run at various depths. As a result, three shad-gray crankbaits in shallow-running models, three with mid-depth running capabilities, and three deep-runners amount to nine plugs in the shad-gray color alone. Now add the other five colors in differing depth capabilities, all of them in the three representative body profiles, and it's easy to see how a serious angler can justify reserving an entire tacklebox just to house his collection of perhaps 100 or more crankbaits!

13. Fan-casting is a popular method for fishing crankbaits. In this method, an angler saturates a shoreline point, sunken mid-lake reef, or the S-bend in a stream channel winding along the bot-

Fan-Casting a Point with Crankbaits
(Top View)

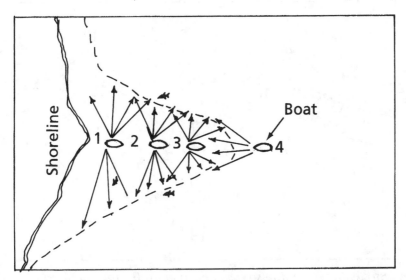

Fan-casting a point with crankbaits is the fastest way to determine if bass are using that structure. Depending on the size of the point, an angler may be able to check it entirely from just one boat position. Or he may have to change the boat position several times and try different crankbaits that run at different depths.

tom with a series of casts in a radial pattern, like the spokes emanating from the hub of a wheel. Once he completes a series of casts, the angler moves his craft slightly and repeats the fan-casting pattern, switching if necessary to a rod rigged with another crankbait that runs slightly deeper. Only the fish can explain why, but it's common for a bass to totally ignore a lure traveling at a certain angle, then blast it on the next cast when the angle of retrieve is changed slightly.

14. A rather stiff graphite rod with a limber tip is best for crankbait fishing. Either an open-face spinning or baitcasting reel is fine. When fishing around vegetation and woody cover, 17-pound-test line is recommended. When fishing "clean" bottom contours or rocky cover, 12- to 15-pound-test line is usually sufficient.

Fan Casting an Old Stream Channel Bend with Crankbaits (Top View)

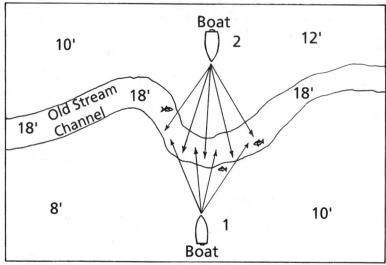

In fan-casting a looping stream channel on the lake floor, two casting positions are sufficient to check it. It might be smart to try several different lure colors, however.

15. If you find yourself in a situation where you don't have a crankbait that runs deep enough to work a given bottom structure, perhaps where your sonar has revealed fish, use the "kneel and reel" method. To do this, cast your lure, then kneel on your seat or on the bow decking, and plunge your rod tip into the water almost up to the reel before beginning the retrieve. This causes the lure to run as much as 10 feet deeper than when standing and casting in the usual way.

16. An alternative to the "kneel and reel" is to carry several sinking crankbaits. With these, you simply cast them out and count them down to the desired running depth; most such lures sink at a rate of approximately one foot per second.

17. A recent survey of tournament anglers revealed that crankbaits with rattles in them outproduce other crankbaits in waters with reduced visibility. A rattle chamber inside a crankbait is nothing more than a tube containing several tiny beads or ball bearings

that make clicking sounds as the lure is retrieved. These alert a bass that something is approaching, and may trigger a response the instant the lure comes within range.

18. In very clear water, on the other hand, crankbaits with interior rattle chambers don't significantly outperform crankbaits lacking such chambers. This is most likely because, in highly transparent water, bass are able to see their prey without having to use their other senses.

19. When fishing around boulders, and especially woody cover such as stumps, logs, and standing timber, use the *bumping* technique. In this technique, an angler casts beyond the cover, begins the retrieve, then suddenly moves the rod tip to one side or the other, causing the crankbait to veer off course, ram into the cover, and just as quickly glance off. No one knows why, but this method often causes a bass to instinctively strike.

20. *Stacking the lures* is used to find the depth at which bass are holding when they're relating to weedline edges that border very deep water, and especially when bass are clinging against steep shorelines where sheer rock walls drop off abruptly into the depths, as in the case of highland and canyonland reservoirs. Position your boat close to the weedline or rock bluff (just a yard or two away) and cast parallel to it, first using a crankbait designed to run two to four feet deep. Next switch to a rod rigged with a crankbait that runs six to eight feet deep. Finally, switch to a crankbait that runs at the 10- to 12-foot level, systematically working deeper and deeper. If you don't find any bass, relocate the boat 30 yards down the shoreline and repeat the maneuver.

21. Many anglers like to just cast a crankbait and steadily reel it in. You'll get much better results by cranking it down to its designed running depth, then momentarily stopping it, and then using a slow pull-and-pause cadence for the remainder of the retrieve.

22. Just because crankbaits have two or three treble hooks, don't be shy about casting them in and around sparse weedbeds and brush. When you periodically snag the lure on a lily-pad stem or the tip of a bush or branch, stop the retrieve immediately, then quickly sweep the rod and rip the lure from the cover. If a nearby bass has been watching the perceived baitfish and sees

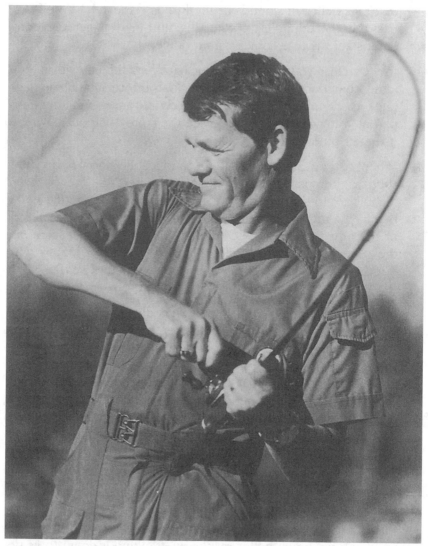

When target casting to stumps and standing timber, many anglers intentionally bump the crankbait against the cover. This can often trigger an involuntary reflex strike from a bass.

it pause and then suddenly begin streaking away, the bass is likely to nail it just as the lure breaks free.

23. You may discover that your crankbait is no longer tracking a straight course on the retrieve, and that it may even roll over and slide to the surface. This is usually due to repeatedly dig-

In addition to crankbaits that dive on the retrieve, a versatile angler carries a selection of slow-sinking lures. Neutral-buoyancy lures (shown here) remain at the same depth level when there is a pause in the retrieve.

ging into the bottom or bouncing off cover. In fact, many brand-new lures don't run properly on the first cast, due to the vagaries of mass production. In either case, the crankbait needs to be tuned. Do this by taking a pair of needle-nosed pliers and bending the wire line-tie loop or eyelet on the lure's nose. If the lure consistently angles off to the right on the retrieve, slightly bend the wire loop or twist the eyelet screw to the left, or vice-versa if the lure veers off to the left.

24. In certain situations, some anglers purposely "untune" their crankbaits to intentionally make them travel at acute angles to the line of retrieve. They do this when fishing docks, places along the banks where trees have low branches extending out over the water, or shorelines where there are underwater ledges and recesses. By bending the line-tie far to the right or left, you can make the lure travel far back underneath such cover in a manner that would be impossible with a tuned lure that tracks a straight course on the retrieve. Get a lure underneath and far back in those dark hideouts, and your chances of finding a really big bass are greatly increased.

25. The best rod for fishing a topwater bait (surface plug) is a medium-action graphite model with a limber tip. Either an open-face spinning or baitcasting reel loaded with 12- to 15-pound-test line is sufficient.

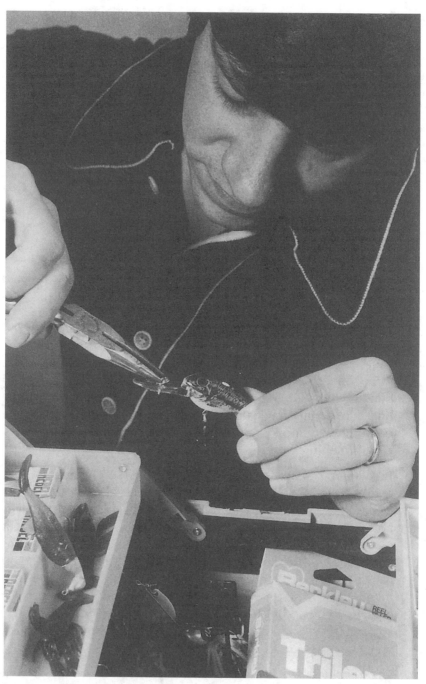

If your crankbait is not tracking a straight course on the retrieve, it needs to be tuned. Do this by bending the line-tie in the direction opposite that in which the lure is running.

Using an Untuned Crankbait to Fish Underneath a Floating Dock (Top View)

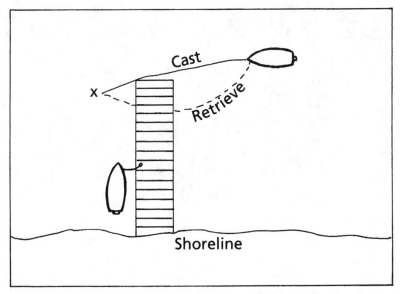

Bass anglers frequently "untune" their crankbaits so they will travel far to one side or the other and into hard-to-reach places that straight-running lures can't reach.

26. The most effective, and popular, topwater plugs are ones that resemble baitfish or frogs. The best time to fish them is when the water temperature is 60°F or higher.

27. Many topwater plugs have a single propeller blade either fore or aft; these are intended for use in cloudy or lightly colored water. Topwater plugs that have tandem propeller blades (fore and aft) are better suited to muddy water or whenever the surface is wind-chopped.

28. Cigar-shaped topwater baits with no propeller blades, such as the venerable Zara Spook, usually produce better results when the surface is calm and flat. Poppers and chuggers, which have concave faces that make popping or gurgling sounds when retrieved, also work best when the surface is calm.

Topwater plugs with either single or tandem propeller blades are best suited for off-colored water or choppy surface conditions.

Cigar-shaped topwater lures such as the Zara Spook make very little noise on the retrieve and are most effective when the surface is flat and calm.

Chuggers can be effective under calm or choppy surface conditions, depending upon how loudly the angler chooses to retrieve them.

29. After casting a surface plug, allow it to lie quietly until the ripples and concentric circles die away. The reason for this is that when a baitfish senses that a predator is near, it will attempt to flee, often by jumping clear of the surface; when it lands, it experiences a momentary shock from the impact, hovering motionless on or near the surface and appearing highly vulnerable.

30. When you begin to retrieve a topwater bait, keep in mind that bass are predators that quickly home in on prey items that appear isolated or disabled. Therefore, an important aspect of fishing such lures is to work them in an erratic manner.

31. Surface lures are by far the most effective at dawn and dusk, especially on bodies of water subjected to heavy fishing pressure or where pleasure boaters and water skiers churn the water and roil the shallows during daytime hours.

32. One instance in which topwater baits can be very effective during midday is on small bodies of water where fishing pressure is light or non existent and there are no other boaters in the vicinity. Another time is during the summer and fall on large lakes and reservoirs, where boating traffic is widely dispersed

and suspended schooling bass periodically charge into schools of baitfish swimming at the surface.

33. On lakes and reservoirs with heavy boat traffic, consider fishing after sunset. Bass actively forage in the dark, so plan to be on the water, at your intended fishing area, about an hour before the sun sets. This will allow your eyes to gradually adapt to the receding light level.

34. If you plan to fish after dark, rig several rods ahead of time and have your gear organized and close at hand. This way you won't have to repeatedly turn on a flashlight to attend to various matters and thus destroy the night vision you've acquired; it may take ten minutes or longer for your eyes to readapt to the darkness after you turn off your light. If there is a substantial level of moonlight, it may not even be necessary to turn on a flashlight.

35. After dark, always leave on your red-green bow light and white stern light, whether motoring from one location to another or when actually fishing. This important safety measure will identify your presence to other anglers on the water. The red-green bow light won't destroy your night vision, but try to avoid looking at the white stern light, which will have the same blinding effect as a flashlight.

36. One hotspot for pitching surface baits after dark is a large mid-lake area, perhaps no more than 15 feet deep, where thick weeds layer the bottom and grow up to within several feet of the surface. During midday, the largest bass in such areas will be buried in the weeds near the bottom, but after dark they rise up to watch overhead potholes and channels in the salad. Begin a drift on the lee side of the weedbed and randomly pitch topwater baits; even though you won't actually be able to see the potholes, your lure will pass over many of them. After completing a drift, motor back to the lee side of the weeds and begin another drift from a different starting point, to cover new water.

37. It may seem logical to use a light-colored topwater plug at night, so bass can see it better. But the opposite is actually true. Solid black is by far the best color to use at this time, as nighttime is rarely totally black. Particularly if there is any degree of moonlight, bass looking up at a surface plug will see it silhouetted

When bass are charging into schools of baitfish on the surface, the action can be so fast that it's not unusual to catch two bass on a single cast.

against the sky; a black-colored lure makes the silhouette even more visible.

38. Some places that ordinarily might not be good spots to find bass during daylight yield impressive action after dark. One such spot is a beach; since the bottom is sandy and free of cover, bass find it easy to force baitfish into the shallows, corral them, and then forage on them.

CHAPTER 14

37 Tips for Fishing Spinnerbaits and Buzzbaits

Use these exciting lures to gurgle, sputter, and churn your way to big bass in heavy cover.

1. Spinnerbaits are among the world's most versatile lures for all bass species. They can be worked through the surface film, throbbed along at mid-depth, or pumped up and down across the bottom. They can be retrieved at speeds ranging from agonizingly slow to intermediate or moderately fast. With such a wide range of depth and speed controls at your command, these lures can be used virtually every month of the year in which there is open water.

2. The spinnerbait is an enigma because it doesn't closely represent anything that bass eat. The attractiveness and strike-triggering ability of the lure can be traced to its flash, action, color, and vibrating sound, which give the illusion that it's alive and trying to get away.

3. By description, a spinnerbait is a combination jig and spinner, with a wire shaft that looks somewhat like an open safety pin. On the lower arm of the wire is a jig head adorned with a rubber or vinyl skirt. On the upper shaft are one or two spinnerblades; spinnerbaits with just one blade are called *single-spins*, and those with two blades are called *tandem* spinnerbaits.

4. The most advanced spinnerbaits have wire shafts made of titanium. No matter how many times the shaft is bent from contact with cover, it instantly snaps back to its original shape; this eliminates the need to occasionally straighten and re-tune the spinnerbait with pliers.

5. If you're using a spinnerbait with a conventional steel shaft, and you have to straighten the wire and re-tune the lure, remember that the upper arm should be in near-perfect alignment with the hook below. The lower wire arm should also be in near-perfect alignment with the hook directly behind the lure head. If a spinnerbait is not tuned properly, it won't travel in an upright position but will tend to either corkscrew on the retrieve or roll over on its side and come to the surface.

6. Most veteran anglers own dozens of spinnerbaits in a wide variety of colors and sizes. The most popular variety among tournament pros is the one-quarter-ounce single-spin. However, it's wise to carry other spinnerbaits in one-eighth- to three-quarter-ounce sizes to meet varying conditions. Use the smaller lures when the water is clear and the larger sizes when the water is murky or off-colored.

Spinnerbaits don't represent anything that bass eat, but they are the most versatile bass lures. Work them slow, fast, shallow, deep, in warm water or cold.

Spinnerbaits are basically nothing more than a jig head with a skirt and an attached wire arm with one or two blades. Some anglers dress the hook with pork rind or a curlytail grub. Countless other variations include head and skirt colors, and the number, size, and color of the blades.

To keep your spinnerbaits organized, use a tacklebox devoted specifically to them. Keep replacement skirts and blades in the box as well.

7. Spinnerbaits come in a multitude of colors with either matching or contrasting colored skirts. The most popular among bass and bass anglers alike are all-white, all-black, all-yellow, all-chartreuse, yellow and black, and chartreuse and black. If some of the lures have single copper blades, tandem copper blades, single nickel blades, and tandem nickel blades, it's easy to see that an avid spinnerbait angler may have as many as 100 of these particular lures at any given time.

8. Change spinnerbait colors often during the day. If one color is producing, but then bass suddenly stop striking, the fish may still be feeding but something may have changed. Cloud cover, for example, may have darkened the light to the point where bass can no longer see a particular color very well. The same is true if you've been casting spinnerbaits in weedy cover, with bass seeing the lure against a green background. If you begin casting around woody cover, the bass may not see the lure very well against the brown or black background.

Most bass anglers prefer vinyl skirts over rubber skirts. The vinyl remains flexible much longer, even in cold water, and the individual strands don't fuse together in warm storage conditions.

9. Opinions vary as to whether rubber skirts are better than vinyl skirts. If the spinnerbait is new, the skirt material doesn't seem to matter. However, vinyl skirts remain flexible and lifelike much longer than rubber skirts, which can become hard and stiff. Rubber skirt strands may even fuse together while in storage in warm temperatures.

10. Some manufacturers assemble spinnerbaits with straight skirts that yield a tight wiggling action on the retrieve. Many anglers reverse these skirts by pulling them off the hook, turning them around, and putting them on backwards. In this manner the skirt no longer trails out far behind the lure but bunches up, giving the spinnerbait a more compact, fuller-bodied appearance. This yields two advantages: When using a slow stop-and-go retrieve, the skirt pulsates like a breathing creature; also, when bass are not aggressively feeding, they have a tendency to just grab the very end of a long, trailing skirt, thereby missing the hook.

11. On days when bass are short-striking, consider adding a trailer hook, sometimes also called a *stinger*. This is a second hook, usually a long-shanked ⅘ Sproat with a wire weedguard, that is

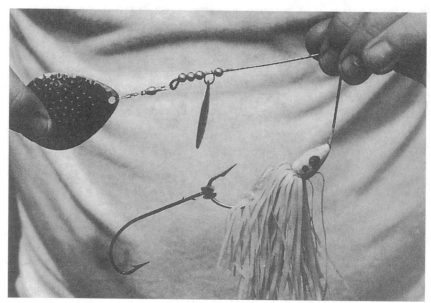

On days when bass are short-striking, rig a stinger hook. Whether the hook point should be up or down is a matter of personal preference.

merely slipped over the spinnerbait hook. Some anglers prefer the hook point to ride up while others like it to face downward. Experiment with both before deciding which style to use.

12. When using a stinger hook, add a "keeper" to prevent the trailing hook from falling off during the cast. A keeper also prevents the stinger from riding up or down the spinnerbait's hook shaft, lodging in place, and affecting the lure's action. Make your own keepers by punching one-quarter-inch circles from plastic coffee-can lids; make about 100 and store them in a little plastic bag. One of these disks can be impaled onto the spinnerbait hook bend, the stinger slipped into place, and then a second keeper disk impaled and pushed down snugly on the eye of the stinger to hold it in place. Another option is to take a length of thin neoprene tubing, cut it into one-eighth-inch-long sections, then thread one onto the spinnerbait hook shaft below the stinger and another above.

13. Always select spinnerbaits that employ the use of ball-bearing swivels in the attachment of the rearmost blade to the upper shaft arm; in a tandem spinnerbait, the other blade is attached

to the shaft by means of a clevis with single ball bearings on either side of the clevis arms. In both cases, the ball bearings allow the blades to turn rapidly, even at the slowest retrieve speeds. When compared to cheap, generic swivels, they are not quickly rendered inoperative when fouled with a bit of weed material.

14. A given spinnerbait may come equipped with several types of blades, each intended for a specific purpose. Colorado blades are nearly round and, when retrieved across the surface, cup maximum amounts of air and force it underwater to create a gurgling noise.

15. Indiana blades are more oval in shape and do not make as much noise on the retrieve. They're ideal for clear-water conditions in which excessive lure noise may spook fish.

16. Willowleaf blades are long and slender. They don't displace as much surface water to make loud gurgling sounds, but do make a lot of underwater vibration. Some multipurpose tandem spinnerbaits are outfitted with a Colorado blade up front and a trailing willowleaf blade. Single-spin and tandem spinnerbaits with willowleaf blades are especially popular with anglers fishing for Florida bass because they come close to representing golden shiners, which are the Florida's primary forage.

17. In ultra-clear water, bright nickel-plated blades are notorious for spooking bass; it's better to switch to spinnerbaits with hammered-brass or copper blades when fishing under such conditions. When the water is cloudy, muddy, or stained, you need additional "flash" to make the lure more visible; now is the time to put on a lure with nickel-plated blades.

18. Deciding whether to use a single-spin or tandem spinnerbait usually depends on the water temperature and whether submerged cover is present. A single-spin sinks more quickly and therefore runs deeper on the retrieve than a spinnerbait with tandem blades does. When cold water requires a slow retrieve, a tandem-bladed spinnerbait is the choice because it can be worked slowly without sinking as deep and getting buried in weeds or brush.

19. Deciding whether to use a single-spin or tandem spinnerbait also depends upon the water color. A spinnerbait with a single blade moves more water than tandem blades (which oppose

each other and somewhat negate their water-moving ability); this makes a single-spin far more effective in off-colored water where a loud, noisy lure helps bass home in upon their target.

20. In addition to using a spinnerbait with its factory-equipped skirt, many anglers like to add embellishments. One is dressing the hook with a twin-tail pork frog or pork eel. Another is removing the skirt and replacing it with a two-inch plastic grub or a twister-type tail. In either case, when bass are in a neutral behavior stage and are short-striking or quickly ejecting a lure, the soft "meaty" texture of the pork or plastic causes them to hold on just a bit longer, thus increasing your odds of a successful hook-set.

21. There are countless ways to fish spinnerbaits. When working them near the surface, many anglers like to hold their rod tip high and reel quickly so the lure's blades are breaking through the surface film. This technique works best in warm shallows (less than six feet deep) where the bottom is littered with heavy weed or wood cover. If the water is cool, better results come from retrieving spinnerbaits a bit more slowly so their blades don't break the surface film but cause a distinct "bulge" just below it.

22. When fishing weeds that heavily mat large surface areas, first fish the perimeter edges and any indentations. Then ease your boat up close to the edge of the weeds and cast far back to any potholes or channels. Don't cast directly into these openings as that will spook a bass that is watching the opening for a prey item. Instead, cast several yards past the pothole, slowly skitter the spinnerbait to the edge of the opening, then stop the retrieve and allow the lure to tumble into the hole.

23. When retrieving spinnerbaits in moderately deep water (eight to 12 feet deep) where cover is poking above the surface (dock pilings, trees, stumps), cast past the obstruction and then move your rod tip right or left so the lure passes close to the cover. If you receive no strike, cast again and begin your retrieve. This time, just as the lure comes next to the cover, stop reeling and allow the lure to slowly flutter-sink to the bottom. If you still do not receive a strike, cast yet a third time and move your rod tip sharply right or left on the retrieve so the spinnerbait actually bangs into the obstruction. When bass are in a neutral behavior

stage, this sudden change in the lure's speed and direction will often trigger a strike.

24. When retrieving spinnerbaits in still deeper water (12 to 20 feet deep), with cover littering the bottom, cast the spinnerbait and turn the reel's handle to engage the gears, but don't immediately begin the retrieve. Instead, let the lure slowly "helicopter" to the bottom on a tight line. Then begin the retrieve, not by reeling but by slowly lifting the rod tip. When the rod tip is at the vertical position, lower it so the lure helicopters downward again. Reel in the slack line that this maneuver generates. Most strikes will occur when the lure is slowly sinking or at the very moment you begin lifting it upward again.

25. Another spinnerbait retrieval tactic for use in moderately deep water where there are felled trees on the bottom is called *slow-rolling*. With this method, the lure is cast and allowed to sink all the way to the bottom before the retrieve is begun. The instant you feel the lure contact the woody cover, stop the retrieve. Then, using your rod tip, slowly "feel" the lure over the obstruction. This will cause it to momentarily turn on its side as it

Slow-rolling and helicoptering are two useful spinnerbait retrieves that serious anglers should know.

passes over the log or tree, thus simulating the way baitfish slide over such obstructions.

26. Most anglers think of spinnerbait fishing in terms of shallow eutrophic natural lakes and flatland reservoirs. But spinnerbaits can also be used in the very deep water (deeper than 20 feet) commonly found in mesotrophic natural lakes, highland reservoirs, and canyonland reservoirs. They're quite effective along steep, rocky shorelines when cast perpendicular to the bank and then slowly "walked" into the depths. This is done by allowing the lure to helicopter downward on a tight line to the first ledge or shelf, then pulling it off the obstruction and letting it free-fall down to the next staircase ledge. As you go progressively deeper, pay out slack line now and then; otherwise, the lure will swing in pendulum fashion back toward the boat and out of the bass' strike range.

27. When fishing very clear deep water, where a small spinnerbait is called for, you can maintain better control of your lure by adding a small split-shot to the lower wire arm just ahead of the jig head. This increases the weight of the lure without increasing its body size.

28. Straight shaft spinners that average two to three inches in length and weigh one-eighth to one-quarter ounce should also be part of your lure selection. Most have an elongated, tubular body shape and a single Indiana or willowleaf blade attached just behind the line-tie on the wire shaft. Although there are a few exceptions, most are outfitted with a single treble hook that is dressed with squirrel-tail fur, bucktail, feathers, or a vinyl skirt. These are basically shallow-water (less than six feet deep) lures best fished with open-face spinning tackle. In larger lakes and reservoirs, use them primarily in the spring when the forage base is small. They're also excellent year-round lures in small rivers and streams where minnows, dace, chubs, and shiners remain relatively small for their entire lives.

29. Buzzbaits are second-generation spinnerbaits that are effective for all species of bass. Take a conventional spinnerbait, lengthen the lower wire arm so the leadhead and hook ride much farther back, substitute an oversize propeller-shaped blade for the Colorado blade, and you've got a buzzbait.

30. Most buzzbaits have flat, wing-shaped blades whose tips turn downward at right angles, a feature that allows them to cup

Buzzbaits are similar in appearance to spinnerbaits. The main difference is their wide-winged blades, which make far more noise than spinnerbaits. They are also fished exclusively on the surface.

large quantities of air and force it underwater to create loud gurgling and buzzing noises. Some buzzbaits have three blades mounted on the wire shaft in pyramid fashion. Others have two angled, stand-up wires emanating from the leadhead, each outfitted with propellers that spin in counter-rotating directions for maximum noise-making and stability on the retrieve.

31. Buzzbaits are available in the same basic sizes and color combinations as spinnerbaits, and their hooks are dressed with the same types of skirts. Unlike with spinnerbaits, you shouldn't substitute a pork or plastic trailer for the skirt, as this makes the offering too unwieldy for casting distance and accuracy.

32. Buzzbaits make far more noise than spinnerbaits. This racket not only seems to attract bass out of deep water and heavy cover, but also provokes violent strikes.

33. Unlike a spinnerbait, which requires furious cranking of the reel handle to keep it topside, a buzzbait instantly rises to the surface and stays there, even at the slowest retrieve speeds. Conversely, if a very fast speed is called for, a buzzbait can easily take it in stride and all the while continue to churn water and

Fish buzzbaits in and around heavy vegetation when the water is warm, and be prepared for explosive strikes.

track a straight course. Spinnerbaits won't do this; retrieve them too quickly and they'll begin corkscrewing or lying down on their sides and veering far off to the right or left.

34. Since buzzbaits are strictly surface lures, and since they typically are retrieved at moderate to fast speeds, use them only when the water temperature is relatively warm. If the water is below 60°F, a buzzbait's effectiveness dramatically falls off.

35. Because of the significant amount of prop-wash that buzzbaits churn up, they're most effective when the water is murky or off-colored. They are somewhat less effective in clear water.

36. Buzzbaits can be fished in the same types of weedy or woody locations where one might surface-fish a spinnerbait. But they're also deadly when fished around docks, piers, and logjams where bass are deep within the cover or far back underneath it. Since a buzzbait closely mimics a large injured shad flitting about the surface, it has the ability to "call" bass out of their normal strike zone.

37. After considerable use, both spinnerbaits and buzzbaits show signs of wear and tear, especially on the skirts and blades. Since both are easily replaceable, it's wise to keep a variety of spares in your tacklebox.

15

38 Secrets to Effective Jig Fishing

Jigs are the only lures found in U.S. military survival kits. Enough said?

1. Jigs can be fished any month of the year, even through the ice. They can be fished shallow, by swimming them just over the tops of submerged vegetation. They can be fished at intermediate depths with a pull-and-pause technique. And they can be fished right on the bottom, at depths to 40 feet or more. Jigs can also be fished at all speeds, ranging from very slow to fast, making them among the most versatile lures for all species of bass.

2. A jig is nothing more than a single hook with an upturned line-tie. Molded around the line-tie, where the hook shank bends upward to form the eye, is a glob of lead that can be of any number of different shapes for the intended purpose.

3. A jig may have a dressing, both to hide the hook and also to create the full-bodied illusion of a live creature. In most cases the dressing consists of bucktail hair, marabou feathers, mylar strands, silicone strands, or a vinyl skirt. The least preferred among bass anglers is the bucktail dressing; the others have much greater bass appeal because they pulsate like a live, breathing creature when the jig is manipulated.

4. Other dressings commonly used to adorn jig hooks include live baits (primarily minnows, leeches or nightcrawlers), pork baits, and plastic curlytail grubs, lizards, and crayfish.

5. Jigs are so simple in construction and materials that many anglers buy jig molds, jig hooks, and an electric ladle, and then melt down old wheel-balancing weights and cast their own jigs.

6. The most popular colors for jig bodies and dressings are all-brown and all-black. Especially when a porkrind or plastic crayfish is added to the hook, those colors ensure that the offering closely resembles a favorite food of all of the bass species. Whether you make your own jigs or buy them commercially, be sure that the dressing on the hook shank contains a bit of orange, which imitates a crayfish's claw joints and underside.

7. The next most popular jig-body and jig-dressing color is white. When a soft white curlytail grub is added to the hook, it's a near-perfect representation of a baitfish.

8. Other jig colors may elicit action from time to time, depending on water color and conditions. Red and black, black and yellow, all-blue, and all-yellow jigs of various sizes should be in every serious angler's tacklebox. As with most other bass lures,

Jigs can be fished any month of the year, in shallow water or at extreme depths, and at a wide range of speeds.

6 Most Popular Jig-Head Designs

Round Ball

Banana

Stand-Up

Football

Keel-Head

Slider

Jigs are often described as merely globs of lead molded around hook eyes. They actually come in a wide range of body styles, each intended for a specific purpose.

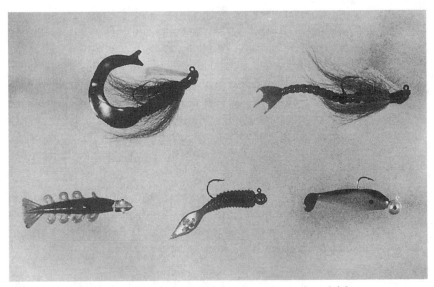

Jigs are not intended to be fished solo. They should have some type of plastic, fur, or skirt dressing to give them a full-bodied appearance.

One of the most popular jig dressings is some type of pork-rind trailer, such as a salamander, split-tail eel, or frog.

pale or subdued colors are usually best in clear water, while dark, bright, or gaudy colors get the nod in off-colored water.

9. Many styles and brands of jigs are specifically designed to mimic baitfish and are sold bare (without a hook dressing of any kind). Instead, a type of molded "keeper" is found at the rearmost part of the jig head, so that a curlytail grub or other plastic trailer can be added and held securely in place. Impale the jig's hook point into the center of the nose of the plastic lure, push it down through the center of the lure body for about an inch, then bring the point out of the side of the lure body. Finally, push the body of the grub up the jig-hook shank until the keeper is buried within the head.

10. Ideally, jigs for bass fishing should weigh somewhere between one-quarter and one-half ounce, although in some applications (when fishing very deep water or fishing for Florida bass) three-quarter-ounce jigs may be brought into play.

11. The three most popular jig-hook sizes are 3/0, 4/0, and 5/0.

12. The two most popular jig-hook designs are heavy-duty Sproat hooks, which have a wide throat (hook bend) to accommodate

bulky pork and plastic dressings; and thin-wire Aberdeen hooks, intended for use with live baits and smaller plastics.

13. There are many jig-head body styles on the market, each intended for a particular fishing application. The round ball design sinks quickly and is intended for vertical jigging for suspended fish or working snag-free bottom contours such as ledgerock dropoffs and gravel reefs. It's also commonly used with live baits. One drawback of the round ball design is that it hangs up easily. Some types of round ball jigs have an attached wire arm and spinnerblade, causing them to somewhat resemble spinnerbaits; they're intended for working weedline edges and other shallow cover such as stumps.

14. The banana-head body style looks like—surprise—a banana. It sinks fairly fast and can more easily be climbed over bottom roots, tree limbs, and light brush cover. It's also a good jig design for working rocky shorelines and dropoffs.

15. The stand-up jig does exactly as its name implies. It is pyramid-shaped, with most of its weight centered on its flat bottom. When it's on the bottom, the hook is always standing upright at a 45-degree angle. This feature makes the jig snag-resistant and, with the point more exposed, setting the hook is easier than with some other jig designs. When dressed with a curlytail grub or other soft plastic lure, or a live bait such as a minnow or leech, the presentation looks very much like some aquatic creature nosing down in a tailing or feeding posture, or trying to crawl into some crevice to hide. This is an excellent jig style when the bottom mire is such that a jig may sink into it and disappear from sight. It's also recommended for thin weed growth, light brush, and scattered rocks and gravel.

16. The football-head jig design has a pointed nose that allows it to be snaked through the thickest weeds and woody cover with a minimum of hang-ups. Since the bottom surface is flat, the jig hook remains in an upright position even at the slowest retrieve speeds. This jig-head style is an excellent choice for use with pork. When fished at slow speeds, other jig-head designs cause the pork to fall over on its side.

17. The keel-head jig design looks somewhat like an aspirin that has been flattened into an oval shape. It rides in a vertical position, as though on its edge, and is most often fished with a plas-

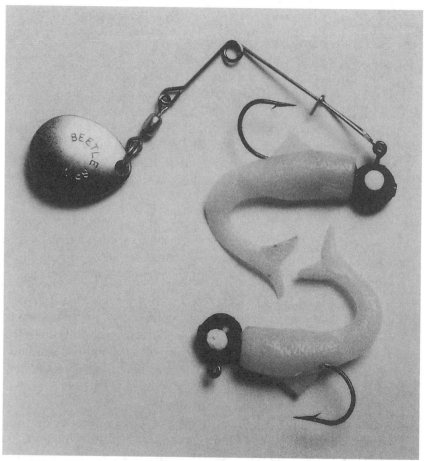

One jig variation comes with a separate wire arm and spinner affair that can be attached or removed as water-color conditions dictate. When used in murky water, the blade adds flash to make the lure more visible.

tic trailer. It's ideal when fishing any water condition, particularly rivers, where there is a current. It's also virtually snag-free in rocky cover.

18. The slider-head jig design also looks like an aspirin, but with a slightly pointed head. It rides in a flattened or horizontal position. This jig design glides and planes through the water in a slow, swimming manner. It's most effective when dressed with a plastic trailer and fished for suspended bass along shoreline bluffs and sheer rock walls.

19. Water temperature determines the type of jig dressing that should be used. If the water is cold (below 60°F), use a pork trailer. If the water is warm (above 60°F), use a plastic trailer; bass are more active in warm water, and plastic trailers are so-called "action" baits.

20. When fishing jigs in thick weeds and woody cover, use a style that has a weedguard. Most of these consist of several stiff nylon strands projecting upward from the top of the jig head and going back at a 45-degree angle to within about half an inch of the point. Since the weedguard strands are flexible, they have little adverse effect on hook setting.

21. When you buy new jigs, take a straight pin and clean out the line-ties before placing them in your tacklebox. Commercially made jigs are dip-painted, and the eyelets are usually filled with paint; cleaning them out at home saves time on the water.

22. Rods and reels suitable for fishing jigs can be either spinning or baitcasting. A medium-action graphite rod with a sensitive working tip will allow the angler to feel the light sensation of a bass inhaling the lure.

23. Generally, 10- to 12-pound-test lines are suitable for all-around jig fishing in waters with a minimum of obstructions, such as highland and canyonland reservoirs and mesotrophic natural lakes. In waters where obstructions are plentiful, such as flat-land reservoirs and eutrophic natural lakes, a better choice is line testing 15 to 20 pounds. In the heaviest cover conditions, as when flipping jigs into potholes in thickly matted weedbeds or into logjams or drowned tree crowns, many anglers go to abrasion-resistant 25-pound-test line.

24. A lower pound-test line, or a line of thin diameter, will cause a jig to sink faster than a higher pound test or thick diameter line. This may be an important consideration under many conditions because bass commonly take a jig on the fall, as it's slowly sinking. Even in clear water, if the water temperature is cold, a higher pound-test line or one of thick diameter may be the best choice; with the bass being less responsive than in warmer water, the slower sinking speed of the jig may elicit more strikes.

25. Jig dressings can also influence the lure's rate of descent. A jig fished only with its factory marabou or mylar dressing will sink faster than a jig dressed with pork, simply because the former

has less water resistance. Jigs dressed with some type of plastic trailer are the slowest sinkers because most soft plastics are impregnated with tiny air bubbles during the injection-molding process.

26. All jigs, regardless of their specific type of artificial dressing, are intended to be cast and retrieved. One exception is when you're vertically jigging beneath the boat, either in standing timber or when working breaks on breaklines. Another exception is when you're flipping jigs into potholes in matted weed growth and into tree crowns and logjams.

27. The flipping technique calls for baitcasting tackle, with the rod about one or two feet longer than that used in conventional lure casting. Most "flips" are gentle casts that travel an average of only 15 to 20 feet. Since they're executed in an underhand casting manner, you have to be standing to make them.

28. The most popular flipping lure is the so-called "jig 'n pig." It consists of a one-quarter-, three-eighth-, or one-half-ounce banana-head or football-head jig in black or brown color, with a black or brown dressing (either mylar strands or a vinyl skirt). A black pork frog is impaled on the hook, although some anglers prefer pork lizards or split-tail pork eels. Always match the right size pork to the jig you're using; the combination is far less effective if the pork is too large or too small. The label on the pork bottle indicates the proper size jig to be used with that product.

29. To flip a jig 'n pig, hold the rod in your right hand and strip about eight feet of line off the reel, so that when the rod tip is held high the lure hangs down and barely touches the water's surface. Next, strip off still another eight feet of line and hold it at arm's length with your left hand (there will be four feet of line going from the rod to your hand, and another four feet going back to the rod). Then simply swing the rod in a soft underhand manner so the lure rocks like a pendulum and sends the jig toward your intended target. Just as you make the "flip," release the line being held in your left hand. The instant the jig contacts your target, quickly engage the reel's gears and gently work the lure in place. Next, grab the line at the first guide (closest to the reel), pull it back and far to your left side while simultaneously raising the rod tip to pull the lure out of the hole and begin a second pendulum action to flip the lure to the next target. Expert anglers can repeatedly flip a jig into places

The Bass Angler's Almanac

Many bass tournaments have been won by anglers using the popular jig 'n pig lure and a long, straight-handled rod. The trick is to flip the lure into tight places.

as small as a tea cup and with such a gentle touch that there is barely a ripple on the surface of the water.

30. Flipping jigs into weedy potholes, tree crowns, and logjams is especially productive during cold-front conditions. At these times,

The most commonly assembled jig 'n pig lure consists of a one-quarter-ounce banana- or football-head jig, in black or dark brown, with a black or brown skirt. The hook is dressed with a black or brown pork frog. When worked along the bottom, this rig is an almost perfect representation of a crayfish.

When flipping jigs into cover that you'd never be able to work with any other kind of lure, use a jig that has a fiber weedguard.

bass bury themselves deep within heavy cover and become neutral or even negative in their feeding activity. To draw a strike, a lure must be presented daintily and right in front of them, which flipping a jig 'n pig accomplishes.

31. Flipping jigs is perfect for catching bass that are holding around the vertical pilings far back underneath docks and piers, where it's nearly impossible to present lures by casting them in the conventional overhand manner.

32. If you've been flipping a jig dressed with pork and decide to switch to a spinnerbait or some other lure for awhile, make sure the pork lure remains moist while it's out of the water. The easiest method is to wrap it in a sheet of water-soaked paper toweling or simply take the pork off the jig hook and put it back into its bottle. If the pork is allowed to dry out, it will become stiff and lack any action in the water.

33. Don't attempt to cast a jig dressed with a live bait such as a minnow, leech, or 'crawler, as you'll either rip the bait off the jig hook or quickly kill it. Always fish live baits with the back-trolling method described in Chapter 12.

In addition to weedy and woody cover, jigs are the answer to fishing man-made cover such as docks and boat slips, where traditional overhand casting is ineffective.

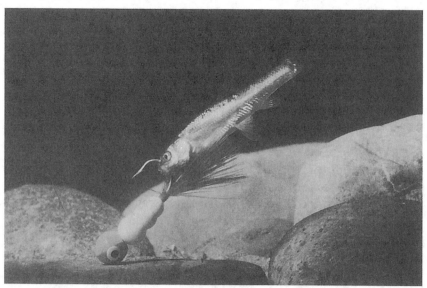

Many anglers, especially smallmouth fishermen, like to dress their jig hook with a live bait such as a minnow, leech, or nightcrawler. Don't cast these, as the bait will be killed or torn off. Instead, use them while backtrolling.

34. Fishing jigs in virtually any type of cover, or along any type of bottom contour, is rather standardized. One thing that's not recommended is merely casting it out and reeling it in, as is done with a spinnerbait or crankbait. Bass don't strike hard when taking a jig; they merely inhale it. To detect the almost imperceptible *bump* or *tap* of a lightly-taking fish, an angler consequently has to rely on the sensitivity of his rod tip; reeling in a jig will destroy that sensitivity, and you won't be able to detect strikes.

35. An optically brightened line that appears to glow above the surface can increase any angler's number of successful hook-ups. Many times a bass strike on a jig is so light that even a highly sensitive rod tip cannot detect it. But you can often see such strikes if you focus on the spot where the line enters the water during the retrieve. If you see the line just slightly twitch, jump, quiver, or move sideways a bit, quickly lean forward, reel in any slack line, and strike! Likely as not, a bass has inhaled your jig, even though you didn't feel a thing.

When a bass inhales a jig, the strike is often so light that you can't detect it through the rod tip. Use an optically brightened line so you can see strikes you'd never feel.

36. After casting a jig, many anglers like to work it back by raising the rod tip from the horizontal position to the vertical. When the rod tip gets to the 12 o'clock position, they lower it quickly, reel in the slack line, and then continue working the jig only with the rod tip. Remember, a jig has no built-in action of its own, other than the slight fluttering action of the dressing on the tail. Because of this, working the jig with intermittent hops and pauses produces the best results.

37. Water temperature determines the speed at which a jig should be worked. In cold water (below 60°F), barely hobble the jig along with short twitches and brief pauses between each forward movement of the lure. In warm water (above 60°F), sweep the jig off the bottom about two feet, allow it to fall back on a tight line, then jump it forward again.

38. A good way to learn how to fish jigs, and how various jig designs respond under the influence of different rod-tip manipulations, is by lowering a jig over the side of the boat in clear, shallow water. Then dance the jig along with jerks, hops, and sweeps of the rod tip to see how it responds and also to learn the best ways to climb jigs over rocks and tree limbs and through weeds.

50 Ways to Fish Soft Plastic Lures

Collectively, soft plastic baits have won more bass tournaments than any other lure category. Do the bass pros know something you don't know?

1. Soft plastic lures include worms, salamanders, tube lures, crayfish, jerkbaits, swimming shad lures, and floating frogs and mice. Biologists who have studied bass behavior in large aquaria say soft plastic baits are effective because they are silent. They lack the rattles, vibrations, and other sounds that are characteristic of so-called "hard" lures, and this missing element, which frequently conditions bass to be wary, reduces their ability to distinguish between the real thing and potential danger. Moreover, once a bass inhales a plastic lure, its soft body feels like natural food.

2. Many anglers erroneously refer to rubber worms, but the correct moniker is plastic worms. Worms and other soft lures are made of a type of plastic called polyvinyl chloride and contain no rubber whatsoever.

3. As a rule, soft plastic lures work best in warm water. When the water temperature begins to dip below 55°F, they become less and less effective. Only the bass know why.

4. Although largemouths, smallmouths, spotted bass, and Florida bass all strike plastic worms, smallmouths do so less often than the other three. Other soft plastic lures are eagerly taken by all bass species.

5. Plastic worms most suitable for bass angling range from four to 12 inches. Water clarity is the most important factor governing the size an angler selects on a given day. When the water is extremely clear, and the fish are easily spooked, use a very small worm. When the water is murky or off-colored in some other way, you want to produce a large visual stimulus (since such lures make little or no sound) and should choose a longer worm. Six- to eight-inch worms are the most popular among bass and anglers alike.

6. Of the countless plastic worm colors, black seems to be a universal favorite that works consistently for most anglers, in most lakes and reservoirs, under most conditions. Blue and purple tie for second place, with motor oil, red, and pale green tying for third. A rule of thumb is to use a dark-colored worm in dark water, and a light, unobtrusive color when the water is clear and brightly illuminated.

7. While plain nightcrawler look-alikes were all the rage 20 years ago, they have since passed from the angling scene. Today,

Plastic lures are effective because they are silent. Even in heavily pressured waters, bass are less likely to become conditioned to them, as they do with hard lures that make noises.

The most popular soft plastic lure is a dark-colored worm with some type of sickle tail, often in a bright contrasting color.

most anglers prefer worms with wafer-thin curlytails or oversize sickle tails that wiggle and undulate when the worm is being retrieved, or wide flapper-type tails that give a worm a porpoising appearance as it is pulled along.

8. Plastic salamanders average four to six inches in length, with five-inchers being the most popular. Owing to their long tails and four legs, they actually appear to be crawling when slowly retrieved across the bottom. The most popular colors are black, red, and green.

9. Tube lures, which average two to four inches in length, have blunt, rounded heads and skirt-like tails with many lively strands. Since most tube lures represent minnows and other small baitfish, they should be in representative colors such as shad gray, mullet blue, and pale green. Many anglers like to fish the lure as is. Since the tube portion of the lure is hollow, some anglers prefer to pack it with scented cotton or gel.

10. Plastic crayfish represent the real thing, claws and all. The most effective are three to four inches in length and in crayfish-look-alike colors (brown, black, dark orange, purple, dark red).

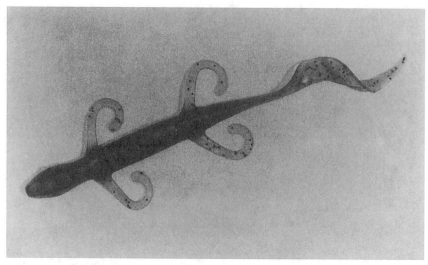

The second-most popular soft plastic lure is the salamander. Its wafer-thin tail and legs give it a lifelike crawling action.

11. The most popular jerkbaits and swimming shad lures are four to seven inches long and come in representative baitfish colors such as light gray, silver, pale blue, and pale green.

12. Plastic frogs and rats average three to four inches in length and are of the same hollow-body design as tube lures except that they're shaped as frogs and small rats and have lifelike legs. The most popular frog color is green with a white belly, while the most popular rat color is black with a white belly. Frogs and rats are the only soft plastic lures that come from the factory already outfitted with hooks, usually a single or double Size 3/0 or 4/0 Sproat hook.

13. Many anglers favor firetail worms, salamanders, and tube lures, in which the tail section is a bright fluorescent color such as hot pink, chartreuse, or orange. The colored tips cause otherwise ordinary plastics to be real attention-getters when the water is off-colored or the fish are in a neutral or inactive state. Similarly, many anglers like to use soft plastic lures impregnated with hundreds of tiny, bright metal flakes in murky water; the glitter reflects any available underwater light and makes the lure easier to see.

14. Hooks for worms and other soft plastics are largely a matter of personal preference. There are two critical things to keep in

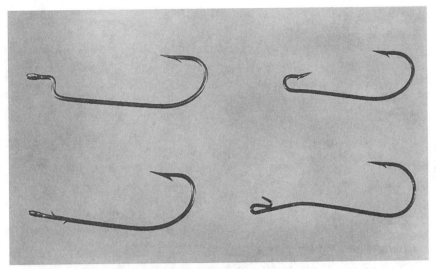

There are many hook styles for use with worms, salamanders, and other soft plastic lures. The choice is up to you; just make sure that the hooks are made of thin wire, but with large enough throats to accommodate the bulky bodies of most soft plastic lures.

mind: 1) Always match the hook size to the lure size (in other words, small hooks for small lures, large hooks for large lures); and 2), stick with needle-sharp, thin-wire hooks that don't damage the relatively fragile lures and are easiest to set and penetrate deeply into a bass' jaw. Aside from this, hook sizes run the gamut from Size 1 to 6/0, the most popular being 2/0, 3/0, 4/0, and 5/0 in long-shanked Sproat and Aberdeen designs.

15. Most worm hooks come from the factory with round, cone-shaped points. Since the hook, upon the strike, must first penetrate the body of the soft plastic lure just to get into position to penetrate a bass' jaw, many anglers like to use a file or stone to rework their hook points into a triangular shape to afford better cutting action.

16. Traditionally, sliding sinkers are used in fishing plastic worms, salamanders, crayfish, and tube lures. These sinkers have holes through their centers, through which the line is first threaded before tying on the hook. The advantage here is that the sinker gives the lure casting weight; yet when a bass inhales the lure and begins to move off with it, line travels freely through the sinker so the fish feels no resistance.

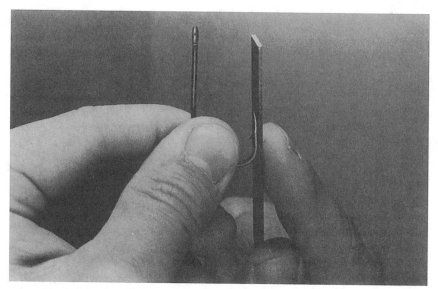

Most hooks come from the factory with cone-shaped points. If you're going to use them with soft plastic lures, sharpen the points into triangles to better penetrate the plastic on the hook-set.

Sliding sinkers allow a bass to pick up a soft plastic lure and move away with it without feeling resistance. Cone-shaped sinkers are more likely to come through cover without hanging up.

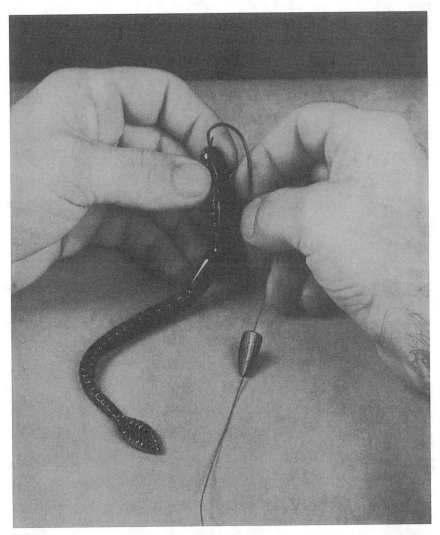

To assemble a Texas-rigged worm, first thread your line through the sinker and tie on the hook. Then impale the hook point through the center of the worm's head.

17. Sinkers that are streamlined and bullet-shaped move through thick cover much more easily than those with wider profiles and that are intended for open-water fishing around reefs, clean drop-offs, and steep shoreline bluffs.

18. Although the size of the sinker should be closely matched to the size of the lure, water depth and wind velocity are even more significant in determining the proper sinker size. The rule

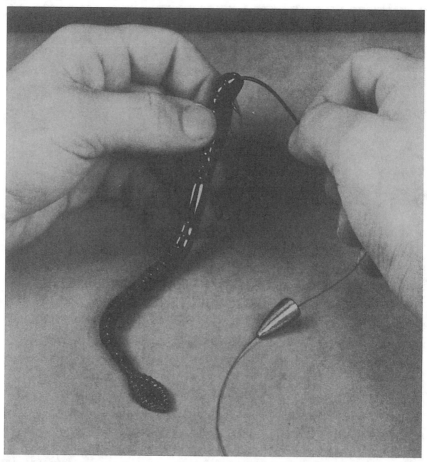

Next, bring the hook point out of the side of the worm, about a quarter inch below the head.

of thumb is to use the lightest sinker possible that will allow you to cast the lure accurately, take it to the bottom, and maintain close contact (feel) with it. Sinkers that weigh one-quarter, three-eighths, and one-half ounce are the most popular for most soft plastic situations.

19. There are many ways to rig soft plastic lures, but most are gimmicks. Guides and tournament anglers rely on two methods, the *Texas rig* and the *Carolina rig,* for hooking worms, salamanders, and crayfish. Tube lures, jerkbaits, and swimming shad lures can be rigged Texas-style, but they're just as often rigged with the hook shank inserted through the length of the

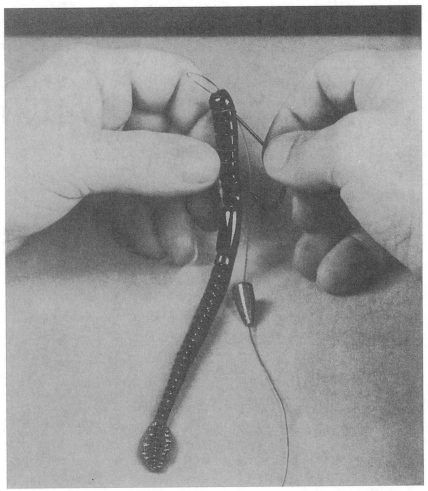

Finally, turn the hook around so the point is toward the worm and bury the point into the plastic almost to the opposite side of the worm body.

body, with the point exiting along the lure's back so it's fully exposed.

20. The Texas rig is made by threading the line through a slip sinker and then tying a hook to the terminal end. The hook point is then pierced through the nose of the lure, brought out the side a quarter-inch lower, reversed, and the tip then impaled back into the plastic to make it weedless. Generally, a slow-sinking or semi buoyant lure is used.

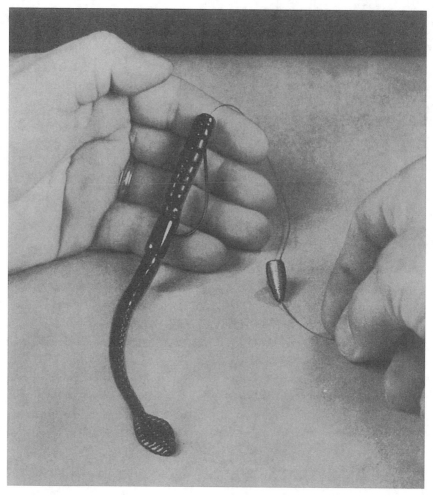

A finished Texas-rigged worm should hang straight; if it's not straight it will corkscrew in the water and twist the line.

21. Anglers use the Texas rig when they want to fish a soft plastic lure right on the bottom across rocks, brush, logs, stumps and other cover.

22. With the Carolina rig, the line is threaded through either a slip-sinker or barrel-sinker in the usual manner, but the terminal end of the line is not tied to the hook but to a small swivel. A two-foot length of line is then tied to the other end of the swivel, the terminal end of that line to the hook, and the lure then impaled in the usual manner to make it snag-free. A high-floating lure should be used with the Carolina rig.

Carolina Rig

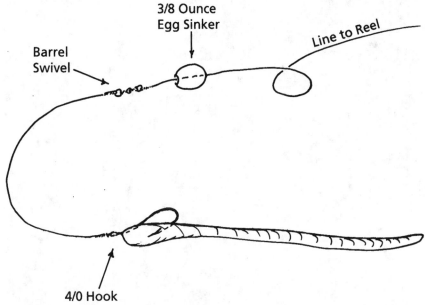

In assembling a Carolina-rigged worm, bury the hook in the plastic the same as you would when Texas-rigging a worm. The difference is that the line is first threaded through an egg sinker and tied to a barrel swivel; a leader is then added, and its terminal end tied to the hook.

23. The Carolina rig comes into use when the bottom is muddy or mucky or there is sparse weed growth. In these situations, a Texas-rigged lure would be constantly buried in mire or otherwise out of a bass's visual range. With a Carolina rig and a high-floating lure, however, the sinker drags bottom while the bait floats about a foot or two above the bottom, remaining in clear view of nearby bass.

24. Hooks specifically designed for soft plastic lures typically have barbs to keep the lure from sliding down the shank. If the shank does not have barbs, slide the head of the soft bait over the eye of the hook and anchor it by pushing a toothpick through the lure and hook eye. Then trim off the ends of the toothpick.

25. Plastic salamanders and crayfish should be rigged Texas style. Because these offerings have bulkier bodies, the hook size must

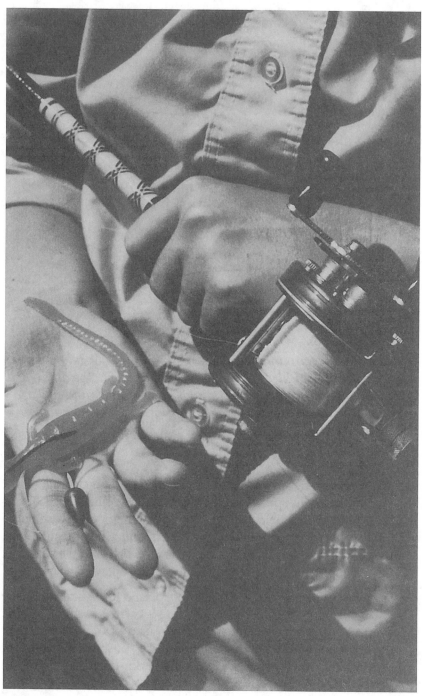

Be prepared for jolting strikes because bass hate salamanders and try to kill them, even when they're not actively feeding.

be at least one size larger than would be used with a worm of the same length.

26. Texas-rigged and Carolina-rigged soft plastic lures, especially worms and salamanders, should always hang straight so they won't corkscrew in the water and twist the line.

27. In working a worm, salamander or crayfish, the lure should always be lifted and pulled with the rod tip, never retrieved by simply turning the reel handle. The basic method is to cast the bait and allow it to sink to the bottom on a tight line (many strikes will come on the fall). When the lure hits bottom, slowly begin lifting the rod tip to move the lure several feet. When the rod tip is pointing vertically upward, drop it quickly, reel in the slack line, stop reeling, then begin lifting the rod tip to again move the bait forward several more feet.

28. Vary the way you work a worm, salamander, or crayfish across the bottom. A lively bait will almost always outfish one that is retrieved in a mundane manner, so try to impart your lure with

When bass are in relatively shallow water, one of the most popular ways to fish plastic salamanders and crayfish is to gently flip them up onto a muddy or gravel bank and then slowly crawl them into the water.

action. One way is to simply shake your wrist now and then, to simulate the appearance of something crawling and gyrating as it tries to pick its way over and through bottom cover.

29. Anglers who are experts at fishing plastic worms, salamanders, and crayfish commonly refer to their rods as "pool cues" or "broomsticks" due to the heavy duty, stiff action of the rod blank all the way from the butt to the tip. When setting the hook, keep in mind that first you have to drive the hook through the plastic in which it's imbedded before it can even begin to penetrate a bass's mouth. A so-called "spaghetti" rod action can't accomplish this, nor will it allow you to muscle the fish out of the heavy cover in which soft baits are usually fished.

30. With a Texas-rigged or Carolina-rigged worm, salamander, or crayfish, many anglers like to push the point of the hook all the way through the bait until it exits the opposite side, and then back it up just a bit so the point is concealed and to make the lure weedless. This also creates a little channel through the plastic, just ahead of the hook point, which makes the hook-setting job is easier.

31. Don't expect arm-jarring strikes when fishing plastic worms or crayfish; the pick-up will just be a *tap . . . tapping* sensation, a barely perceptible bump, or you'll see the line moving sideways a bit. Other times, a bass may inhale a worm and begin swimming toward you, giving a sensation of nothing on the end of your line, as though your lure had been cut off.

32. When a bass inhales a salamander, it's often in a far more forceful manner; bass hate salamanders and try to kill them, even when they're not actively feeding.

33. When fishing any type of soft plastic lure, never get into a feeling contest with a bass, because you'll lose every time. If you feel something happening on the end of your line, quickly lean forward and extend your rod tip toward the fish, so the bass does not detect any resistance. Then simultaneously begin reeling in line and setting the hook with a strong upward sweep of the rod tip, all in one continuous motion.

34. As a rule, tube lures are either Texas-rigged or fished with exposed hook points. Since tube lures are lightweight, they're generally fished with medium-light spinning tackle. Because a lightweight line has more stretch than a heavier pound test, and

because a lightweight line doesn't telegraph a *tap . . . tap . . . tapping* sensation as acutely as a heavier pound test line, it's best to make only short casts. If you keep your casts to no more than about 35 feet, you'll feel more strikes and be more efficient in setting the hook.

35. Tube lures rigged with the hook point exposed, and with a lightweight slip-sinker on the line, are fished essentially the same way you'd fish a jig dressed with a curlytail grub in shallow-water situations. Swim it along by slowly raising the rod tip to the vertical position, dropping the rod tip and reeling in the slack, then raising the rod again. Flick your wrist occasionally to cause the lure to dart forward in short bursts and mimic a baitfish.

36. Tube lures that are Texas-rigged, and with a slightly heavier slip-sinker on the line, should be fished essentially the same as you'd fish a jig 'n pig in deep water. Swim it with long pauses in between each forward movement of the lure, and be sure to occasionally sweep it off the bottom and then let it fall back on a tight line.

37. Plastic worms, salamanders, crayfish, and tube lures can be "flipped" in almost exactly the same manner as jigs dressed with pork, as described in Chapter 15. The best locations for doing this are openings in brushy cover and heavy weed growth such as milfoil, lily pads, and hyacinths. When flipping soft plastics, it's best to peg the sinker against the head of the lure. Simply wedge a round toothpick into the hole on the top of the sinker and trim it flush with nail clippers; don't use a triangular or square toothpick, which might nick the line. Pegging the sinker keeps it from riding up the line and getting snagged in overhead cover.

38. When the standard lift-and-crawl method of working plastics along the bottom isn't producing, use the yo-yo method. Plastic worms, salamanders, and tube lures that are rigged Texas-style with pegged slip-sinkers are best suited to yo-yoing. Simply work the lure vertically up and down the far side of a horizontal branch or tree trunk; the woody cover can be partly submerged or even above the surface. With the rod tip, raise the lure off the bottom, giving it a wrist-shaking jiggling motion. When the head of the lure contacts the cover overhead, pause and then give slack line so it flutter-sinks back to the bottom. Most strikes will come on the fall.

Tube lures and soft plastic jerkbaits are deadly when worked in openings in heavy cover.

39. When fishing plastic worms, salamanders, crayfish, and tube lures along rock walls and bluffs that drop steeply into deep water, keep in mind that most of the bass will be holding tightly against the vertical structure. Be sure that you don't allow the slowly sinking lure to swing in an arc back to the boat and move out of the fish zone. This usually happens when the rod

tip is left in the horizontal position immediately after the cast. Instead, when the lure splashes down, raise the rod tip to the 12 o'clock position without engaging the reel's gears. This will yield slack line. Now engage the gears and begin dropping the rod tip at a slightly faster rate than the descending lure.

40. Have you ever made a poor cast with a plastic lure such as a worm, and then had to spend long minutes picking out a back-lash on your baitcaster, only to finish the work and begin reeling and feel a bass on your line? This apparent oddity is actually so common that it long ago gave birth to the patience-taxing method known as dead-sticking. Simply cast to thick cover (wood is best) and allow the lure to lay motionless on the bottom for at least three minutes. Then just barely twitch it. If a bass has been watching the lure but has been reluctant to take it, right then is when he's likely to do so.

41. Many anglers like to doctor their plastic lures with a scented spray, in the belief that a bass inhaling the lure will not detect some unnatural odor and spit it out before the hook can be set. Use a flavor (shad, crayfish, salamander, earthworm) that matches the style of lure being used, and give the plastic bait an additional shot after every ten casts to keep it fresh.

42. One effective method of fishing plastic worms, salamanders, and crayfish in rivers, where one has to contend with current, is called *slip-corking*. This works especially well where there are logjams and felled trees along the banks. First, thread a cylindrical-shaped cork with a hole running through it onto your line; the cork should be about one inch in diameter and two inches in length. Now assemble a Texas-rigged lure at the terminal end of the line. Position your boat upstream of the cover you intend to fish and begin paying out line so the cork with the worm rig immediately underneath it floats over the cover. Now pay out more slack line until the worm sinks straight down into the cover, and begin working it in place. Watch the cork closely; if it jumps, set the hook.

43. When the water is relatively shallow (less than six feet deep) and there is thick, floating vegetation such as lily pads, use a Texas-rigged worm, salamander, or tube lure without the sliding sinker on the line. A floating or semi buoyant lure is best, and since it will be lightweight without its usual sinker, open-faced spinning tackle makes casting the rig easier. Simply pitch the lure across the matted weeds and allow it to set down and

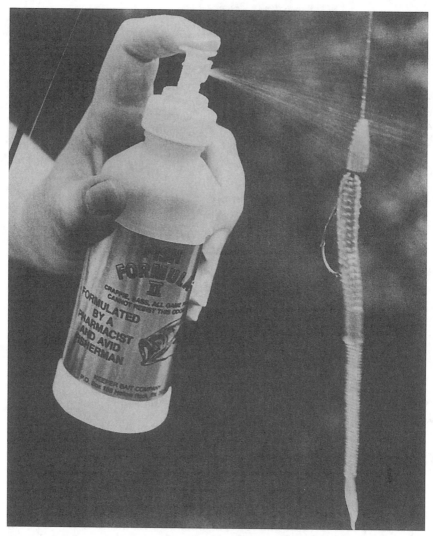

Many anglers like to douse their soft plastic lures with a scented spray. They're available in shad, crayfish, earthworm, and salamander flavors.

rest motionless for a moment. Then begin slowly swimming it along so the tail is able to give a gyrating, crawling appearance. Bass don't gingerly inhale plastics fished in this manner, as they do when the lures are slip-sinkered and retrieved along the bottom, so be prepared for smashing strikes.

44. When the water is relatively shallow (less than six feet deep) and there is weed growth growing up to within several feet of the surface, use a plastic swimming shad lure or a jerkbait such as a Fin-Shad or Slug-Go. Floating or slow-sinking models work best, and they should be rigged Texas-style without slip-sinkers. Simply cast the lure out at random and, by raising and lowering the rod tip, slowly swim it along with occasional pauses, twitches, and jerks. Bass holding deep in the weeds strike these soft lures just as they strike hard surface plugs.

45. Swimming-shad lures and jerkbaits can be fished deep in stumpfields and around sunken rocky islands and reefs. Use a floating model rigged Carolina-style so the baitfish swims just off the bottom.

46. Although spotted bass hit plastic worms just as aggressively as largemouths do, they're more difficult to hook because they have a tendency to strike short, grabbing just the tail section of the lure. Try increasing your hook-ups by using a shorter worm (no more than five inches long). If this doesn't work, rig a trailer hook near the tail by tying a three-inch length of mono to the bend of the front hook and running it to the rear hook.

47. Plastic frogs and rats are most effective in shallow water (less than five feet deep) where there is sparse surface vegetation such as lily pads, submergent vegetation that comes up to within two feet of the surface, or brush and other woody cover laying on the bottom. Mastering the use of frogs and rats is easier than any of the other plastic lures. Simply cast them out and work them back slowly, as you would any other surface lure.

48. When fishing a plastic frog or rat, don't try to immediately set the hook on the strike, as the lure will probably come flying back at you. Bass commonly try to first kill these critters with a rushing, stunning blow, and then return to pick it up as it lies motionless on the surface. Other times, a bass will only partially inhale the critter, then turn it around in its mouth before starting to swallow. In either case, upon getting a strike, count to three before attempting to set the hook. If you're missing fish, begin giving them a five-count.

49. All soft plastic lures are effective after dark, especially frogs and rats because of the noise they make as they are skittered and scampered across the surface.

Plastic frogs and rats come with hooks already attached and don't require sinkers because they're strictly topwater lures intended for skittering across matted surface vegetation. Don't set the hook until you feel solid resistance, because bass first deliver a stunning blow before taking the lure into their mouth.

50. If you cast any type of soft plastic lure and a bass boils the water underneath but doesn't actually take it, or if a bass strikes and misses, immediately follow up with another cast with a radically different lure. This is one reason why tournament anglers always have a selection of rigged rods with various lures tied on. For example, if you miss a bass strike on a blue plastic worm worked deep, follow up quickly with an all-black jig 'n pig. Or if you miss a strike on a silent-running, shad-colored jerkbait, follow up with a noisy, chartreuse buzzbait.

30 Methods for Fishing Weedless Spoons and Jigging Spoons

Spoon-fed bass make for happy anglers. But there's more to fishing these lures than just casting out chunks of heavy metal and reeling them in.

Most weedless spoons are elongated, forged, outfitted with weed-guards, and painted. They're almost always fished with some type of trailer, such as a vinyl skirt, porkrind, pork frog, or soft plastic.

1. Metal spoons are among the oldest artificial lures. They come in two categories: weedless and jigging. Weedless spoons average two to five inches in length, with the most popular weights being one-quarter, three-eighths and one-half ounce. Weedless spoons are intended for shallow-water work (less than six feet deep) and have a weedguard extending from the line-tie back to within a quarter inch of the hook point; the weedguard is usually made of thin wire, plastic, or nylon bristles. Jigging spoons, which are intended for deep-water work, do not have weedguards.

2. The typical weedless spoon is an elongated- or teardrop-shaped piece of thin metal forged into a concave shape so it rocks back and forth on the retrieve. This design, along with the weed-guard, allows the lure to be slithered and skittered over and through both submergent and emergent vegetation with a mini-mum of hang-ups. Weedless spoons can also be worked through sparse woody cover such as brush.

3. Since weedless spoons represent baitfish and amphibians such as frogs, tadpoles, and salamanders, the most popular colors are

nickel, gold, silver, pale green, pale blue, dark-green frog pattern, olive, and black.

4. Most anglers like to dress weedless spoons with some type of tail or skirt to give the lures a more enticing wiggling appearance in the water. Nylon skirts, like those found on spinnerbaits and buzzbaits, are very popular. Generally, the lure is most effective when the spoon and skirt are of contrasting colors, such as a black skirt on a silver spoon, a light-green skirt on a dark-green frog-pattern spoon, or a pale-blue skirt on a gold spoon. Experiment to see what works best on any given day.

5. Bass fishermen also like to dress weedless spoons with pork. Several all-time favorites are: a four-inch white porkrind strip on a silver spoon; a two-inch-long, green frog-pattern pork chunk with a split tail on a silver spoon; and a four-inch, black split-tail pork eel on a black spoon. These soft dressings give the hard metal lures a somewhat meaty texture, causing bass to hold on a bit longer at the strike.

6. When bass are in a neutral or inactive behavior stage and are reluctant to hit other lures, try using a black spoon with either a black split-tail pork eel or a black plastic worm impaled on the hook. This affair closely represents a small water snake. Bass strongly dislike snakes and will try to kill them even when they're not hungry. Remember to keep a proper balance between the spoon and worm size: With a one-half-ounce spoon, use a five- or six-inch worm; with a one-quarter-ounce spoon, use a four-inch worm or a three-inch curlytail grub.

7. Tackle for fishing weedless spoons can be the same spinning or baitcasting gear you'd use with spinnerbaits or buzzbaits. This means a moderately stiff-action rod with a working tip and line testing from 12 to 17 pounds, in accordance with the density of the cover being worked.

8. One of the most explosive methods of fishing for bass is to skitter a weedless spoon dressed with a pork frog through lily pads. Periodically slow the retrieve, lift the rod tip, and gently crawl the lure up onto a floating pad. Let it sit motionless for a minute, gently ease it off the pad and back into the water, and hang on!

9. When fishing a shoreline rimmed with weeds that extend out various distances, observe the curvature of the weedline. It will follow the depth contours because, right at the edge of deep

(Top View)

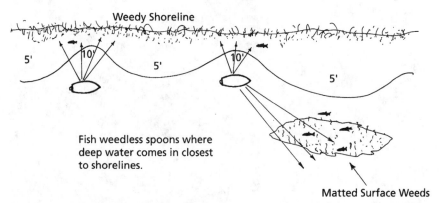

Weedy Shoreline

5'   10'   5'   10'   5'

Fish weedless spoons where
deep water comes in closest
to shorelines.

Matted Surface Weeds

*Weedless spoons are intended for fishing heavy vegetation. Fish shore-
line weeds where the water abruptly drops off, or across potholes in
matted surface weeds.*

water, sunlight penetration is not sufficient to allow weeds to
grow any deeper. Bass will frequently hold along the weedline
where the water is deepest near the shoreline.

10. Another type of edge that bass favor is where two different weed
species meet. Lily pads generally favor a soft, mucky bottom while
reeds, cabbage weeds, and coontail moss prefer a firm bottom.
The point where the lily pads stop and another species takes
over is an edge that bass frequently cling to. Drag weedless spoons
across this edge and you'll likely catch more bass than if you exclusively fished lily pads or some other weed species.

11. When fishing shoreline cover, look for patches of dirt on the
bank where there is no grass growing. Try to cast a weedless
spoon dressed with a pork frog right onto this bare ground.
Then slowly crawl the lure into the water with barely a ripple. If
a bass is nearby, chances are he'll grab it.

12. Jigging spoons are elongated, pencil-shaped or oval-shaped
chunks of steel or lead, some with painted surfaces and others
with hammered finishes. Most have a single treble hook that is
either bare or outfitted with a feather dressing. The most popular sizes range from one-quarter to five-eighths of an ounce.

13. Since jigging spoons are such close representations of baitfish,
many anglers prefer their natural metal finishes (silver, nickel,

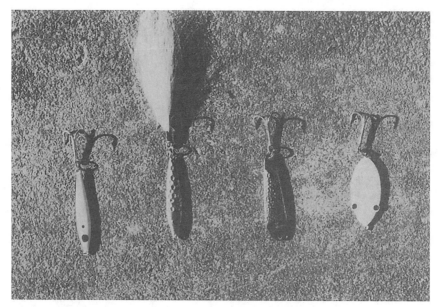

Jigging spoons, often dressed with fur, are designed to be fished vertically beneath the boat, but also can be cast to surface-feeding bass in mid-lake areas.

gold). When moved through the water, the hammered finishes of these spoons simulate the sparkle and flash of smaller fish. These specific finishes and colorations are the wisest choice when the water is stained, murky, or off-colored because they reflect maximum amounts of underwater light.

14. If the water is clear or just slightly milky- or sandy-colored, bright metal jigging spoons may spook bass. Instead, try fishing with jigging spoons with gray, pale-green, pale-blue, and white finishes.

15. Jigging spoons are not meant to be cast in the usual way. They can be cast if necessary, such as when schooling bass are tearing into schools of baitfish on the surface. Due to their compact sizes, they cast like bullets, even into a stiff wind.

16. Typically, jigging spoons come into their own when fished vertically beneath the boat at various depths ranging from five to 50 feet. This makes them among the most popular lures for summer, fall, and winter use on highland and canyonland reservoirs, the deepest tailwater areas of flatland reservoirs, and natural mesotrophic lakes.

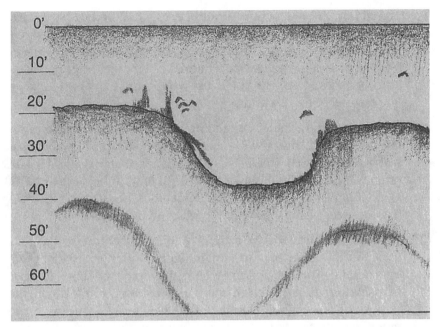

This sonar printout shows bass relating to stumps along the edges of the old riverbed in a flatland reservoir, a situation tailor-made for working jigging spoons.

17. On man-made bodies of water, there are many locations ideally suited to the use of jigging spoons fished vertically beneath the boat. Many anglers like to fish deltas. These are deep sandbars or ridges found along the edges of the old riverbed and associated stream channels on the lake floor.

18. Other locations where jigging spoons are deadly on man-made bodies of water include breaklines (sharp dropoffs) and breaks (intermittent pieces of cover such as stumps) on breaklines. Also try the S-turns in stream channels winding along the bottom, steep shoreline points, and the steep rubble "rip-rap" banks along causeways and on the dam. If there is an elevated highway bridge or railway trestle crossing the reservoir, the supporting pillars are tailor-made for the use of jigging spoons.

19. On natural mesotrophic lakes, use jigging spoons at breaklines, breaks on breaklines, sunken rock-capped islands, gravel reefs, steep shoreline points, and along steep rubble shorelines.

20. Either spinning or baitcasting tackle is suitable for use with jigging spoons. For vertical fishing in heavy cover such as stand-

ing timber, the rod action should be moderately heavy; in fact, the rod you'd select for plastic worm or jig 'n pig fishing is perfect, with line testing 15 to 20 pounds. For casting into surface-feeding action in open-water, mid-lake regions, the same spinning or baitcasting rod you'd use with crankbaits is fine, with line testing 10 to 12 pounds.

21. When casting into surface-feeding action where bass are gorging upon shad, minnows, or other preyfish, most of the bass will be of relatively small size, seldom more than two-and-a-half pounds, and they will be within several feet of the surface. With a moderately fast retrieve, it's sometimes possible to catch a bass on every cast, although the action typically is brief.

22. When small schooling bass are charging prey on the surface, it's common for larger bass to remain deeper, often six to eight feet beneath the surface action, where they pick off mauled baitfish sinking down through the water column. Slow down the retrieve of your jigging spoon and its weight will cause it to run much deeper, to where the larger fish are.

23. There are two standard ways of vertically fishing jigging spoons directly beneath the boat. The first works best in situations that are relatively cover-free. Begin by pressing the baitcaster's free-spool button, or releasing the spinning reel's bail, and allow the line to pay out as the lure sinks to the bottom. Then, with the rod tip just inches above the surface of the water, engage the gears, take up any slack, and begin slowly raising the rod tip in short jerks until the rod tip is pointed at the 12 o'clock position. This maneuver serves to lift the spoon about 15 feet off the bottom. Then slowly lower the rod tip back down until it again almost touches the surface of the water, causing the spoon to rock and flutter like an injured baitfish struggling as it descends into the depths.

24. If the cover-free water is deeper than 15 feet, and your sonar (or gut instinct) tells you bass are suspending well off the bottom, free-spool your spoon all the way to the bottom. Then, with the rod tip nearly touching the surface, quickly reel in about 10 or 15 feet of line before beginning the slow, jerky lifting of the rod tip to work the next higher layer of water.

25. The second jigging method is designed for heavy-cover situations where the water is only moderately deep (10 to 20 feet).

*After locating a bottom structure with sonar, many anglers find they
can more efficiently fish it if they first mark it with floating buoys.*

It's especially effective over drowned timber, such as stumps
on the bottom, toppled shoreline trees, standing timber, or even
logjams. In these situations, the boat can be positioned over the
top of the cover, with the jigging spoon vertically lowered right
down through the limbs, branches, and trunks to bass hiding
deep within the maze of cover. Holding the rod horizontally,

lower the spoon to the bottom and work it in place by pumping it up and down; then reel in several feet of line and repeat the procedure until you've covered all three-foot depth increments up to the surface. Then, without moving the boat, simply drop the spoon right back into some other hole in the cover and try again. There are times when you'll find an almost infinite amount of bass in the thick crown of one treetop.

26. With either of the two jigging tactics just discussed, most strikes will come as distinct bumps as the spoon is sinking.

27. For some reason, jigging spoons fished vertically beneath the boat in woody cover are not very effective at night. On the other hand, weedless spoons fished in and around thick vegetation are deadly after dark.

28. There are times when a jigging spoon's hooks will hang up deep within a latticework of woody cover. If the hook point is imbedded in the bark, or the hook bend is around a branch,

When fishing standing timber with jigging spoons, move the boat right up next to each tree so you can vertically work its entire height from top to bottom.

If your lure becomes hung up, give it some slack, then jiggle the rod slightly.

the problem is easily remedied. Just give a bit of slack line and lightly jiggle your rod tip. This will cause the spoon to begin flip-flopping back and forth, and its heavy weight will eventually dislodge the hooks. Do *not* pull hard on the line, as this will only drive the point deeper into the wood.

29. When a jigging spoon hangs up in rocky cover, it's usually because the lure's nose has become wedged in a crevice. Don't pull hard on the line, as that will only jam the lure more tightly into the niche. Instead, move your boat a short distance to get on the other side of the cover so you can exert line pressure and try to pull the lure back in the opposite direction.

30. Whenever you are able to loosen a snagged jigging spoon and retrieve it back to the boat, check the line carefully for frays. Chances are it will be nicked and gouged, and you'll have to cut back three or four feet of the terminal end and retie your knot.

18

32 Trolling Tips

Trolling is so deadly that it's illegal in tournaments. As you'll see, there's more to this technique than just dragging a lure through the water.

There's a lot of water out there, and the bass could be almost anywhere. Trolling is an effective search-and-find method for locating the fish. Once you find bass, you can keep trolling the immediate area or stop and cast lures.

1. In backtrolling, as described in Chapter 12, an angler runs his boat in reverse to present lures and live baits at extremely slow speeds, directly beneath the boat. While backtrolling can be used any month of the year, it's particularly well suited to cooler water temperatures when bass are less active. Conversely, front-trolling, which is sometimes also called speed-trolling, is exactly

the opposite. In this method, the craft is run forward at a much faster speed; this method is best suited to warmer water temperatures, when bass are much more active.

2. All bass species can be taken by trolling in all types of natural lakes, man-made reservoirs, large rivers, large farmponds, and large strip-mine ponds. Only in streams is trolling virtually impossible.

3. Trolling is one of the most efficient methods of determining what type of structure fish are predominantly using in a given lake region, how deep they are, and what lure speed is best for that particular day. Although some anglers troll exclusively, most look upon it as a search-and-find technique that enables them to quickly eliminate barren water and locate concentrations of bass, whereupon they then cast lures to the fish in the conventional manner.

4. The most suitable tackle for trolling is a rather short, heavy-action baitcasting rod, no more than six feet long, and a levelwind reel. Compared with a soft-action, limber rod, a stiffer rod is more capable of transmitting everything the lure is doing to the angler.

5. With a stiff-action rod, such as those used in plastic worm fishing, it is much easier to tell when the lure begins free-swimming (loses contact with the bottom) or perhaps when it begins violently digging into the bottom (this indicates the wrong size lure is being used, the trolling speed is too fast, or too much line has been let out). With substantial amounts of line paid out behind the boat, a stiff rod action also gives the angler more leverage in setting the hook.

6. Nylon monofilament lines are not suitable for trolling because they are too elastic. They're designed this way to absorb the jarring shocks of anglers casting lures and setting hooks. But when a huge amount of line is paid out, as in trolling, this stretch factor magnifies itself to such an extent that setting the hook becomes difficult.

7. Another reason monofilament is a poor choice for trolling is that it begins to bow from water resistance as more and more line is let out behind the boat. This, in turn, causes an angler to lose depth control of his lures. A crankbait that runs 15 feet deep when trolling 30 feet behind the boat, for example, may run only five feet deep if 90 feet of line is paid out.

8. Serious trollers use braided Dacron line, which has virtually no stretch, and thereby allows consistent depth control of lures at all boat speeds, no matter how much line is paid out. Tie a six-foot monofilament leader to the terminal end of the Dacron with a blood knot.

9. Trolling is generally done over clean bottom contours (your lures would continually snag if you tried to troll through brush or weeds). Because of this 10- to 15-pound-test lines are usually adequate. The monofilament leader should be the same pound test as the Dacron.

10. A conventional bass boat can be used for trolling if it has a bow-mounted electric motor that has a 24-volt, high-thrust capability, but it's not an ideal choice. A 12- to 16-foot aluminum V-bottom boat with a tiller-operated outboard of modest horsepower, or a transom-mounted electric motor, offers much better control when watching a sonar screen and bird-dogging breaklines and other bottom contours.

11. Various types of crankbaits and diving plugs do the lion's share of work in trolling. Since they will be moving at moderate to

The boat used for trolling is more important in this type of bass fishing than any other. The most effective craft is an aluminum V-bottom with a tiller-operated outboard.

Crankbaits are the mainstay in trolling. Have a selection of them that run at various depths, in sizes and colors that represent the lake's predominant forage species.

fast speeds, an angler should have them in representative bait-fish colors and ranging in weight from one-quarter to five-eighths ounce. Whether you use an elongated, slim-minnow diving plug, a "fat plug," or something in between depends on the predominant forage species in the lake.

12. The running depth of a trolled crankbait is determined by the width and/or length of the bill on the nose of the lure. In most cases the maximum running depth of a lure is on the package it comes in. By trolling a lure at very slow speeds, you can make it run shallower than its maximum depth capability. The reverse is not true, however; if you troll a lure too fast, in an attempt to make it run deeper than its designed running-depth level, it will usually flip onto its side and slide to the surface.

13. When trolling, alter the lure speed intermittently by changing the motor's throttle settings. A sudden but brief reduction in lure speed followed by a brief surge will often trigger a strike.

14. Trolling is rarely done in water shallower than four feet deep, simply because the boat itself will spook bass. And trolling is rarely done in water that's deeper than 20 feet, simply because no crankbaits are designed to run deeper than this. The exception to this is when an angler adds weights to the line.

15. Many anglers prepare a tacklebox specifically organized for trolling with individual trays of lures holding plugs of various colors that all run at a specific depth. In other words, one tray may hold lures that all run four to six feet deep, another tray may hold lures that run at six to eight feet deep, and so on. This makes lure changes fast and easy when a trolling-depth change is desired.

16. Trolling can be tiring if you're in an uncomfortable position. Most experts recommend holding your rod in your right hand. Rest the reel and the hand holding the rod in your lap and, with the length of your rod lying on a horizontal plane, brace the butt section of the rod against your knee, allowing the opposite hand to be free for operating the outboard or transom-mounted electric motor.

17. If you plan to troll while seated in the bow of a bass boat, make sure your electric motor has a foot control pedal.

18. One of the most difficult aspects of trolling is knowing how much line to let out behind the boat. As a general rule, if you are trolling in water from six to 12 feet deep, let out approximately 25 yards of line. In water from 12 to 20 feet deep, let out approximately 40 yards.

19. To pay out precisely measured lengths of line, consider buying a reel with a line counter that tells you exactly how much line, in feet, has been let out behind the boat. Most line-counter reels cost less than $100.

20. If you don't want to buy a line-counter reel specifically for trolling, you should meter your line instead. To do this, tie your line to an immovable object and begin walking away while allowing 50 yards or so to peel off the reel spool. Then, using a felt-tipped pen with brightly colored, waterproof ink, make inch-long marks on the line for every yard. When trolling, count the marks as line pays off the reel and you'll know exactly how far your lure is behind the boat.

21. How deep to troll your lures is one of bass fishing's easiest questions to answer. When the water is eight feet or shallower, and especially if there is cover, bass may be at any depth range; in this case, experiment with different trolling depth levels. However, as a rule, when the water is deeper than eight feet, and especially if there is little cover, bass are generally on or very near the bottom—which is where you want to present your lures.

22. When trolling lures near the bottom in water deeper than eight feet, you should frequently feel them ticking the bottom. If they're violently gouging into the bottom, you're either using a lure that runs too deep, or you're trolling too fast. On the other hand, if you never feel your lure ticking the bottom, they're too shallow and are out of the productive fish zone.

23. When trolling, you should continually feel the vibrations of your diving plug through the rod tip. If you are suddenly unable to feel the plug's wiggling action, chances are the hooks have become fouled with weeds or other debris. Reel in, clean the hooks, and resume fishing.

24. Trolling is best suited to rather lengthy bottom structures that are clean or at least relatively free of cover that can snag lures. Examples include drop-offs (breaklines), old roadbeds on the floor of a reservoir, old stream and river channels that are not too curvy, rocky shoreline bluffs that have underwater ledges that stairstep into the depths, large offshore reefs and sunken islands, well-defined weedline edges, and large shoreline points that extend far out into mid-lake areas.

25. Before trolling over a bottom contour, study your topo map or hydro chart to learn the exact size and configuration of the structure. Also check the water depth so you can select a lure that runs at the appropriate level. Until your trolling skills are mastered, it's best to begin working bottom structures that run in a fairly straight direction.

26. A sonar device is invaluable for accurately trolling over a structure. Keeping your eyes on the screen, you'll be able to constantly make slight course corrections to stay over the area you want to fish.

27. Once you have become adept at trolling structures that travel in a straight direction, you can graduate to more complicated structures that are somewhat crooked.

28. More than one trolling pass is often required to completely check a given structure. A wooded shoreline point that extends out into the main-lake basin is a common example. The ideal way to work such a point would be to make three trolling passes. Don't go across the point and through the standing timber, as that would cause lures to snag. Instead, troll along the length of the

Trolling a Wooded Point
(Top View)

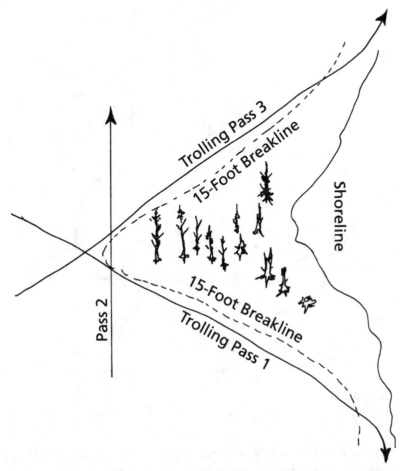

Wooded shoreline points are ideal for trolling. Work the outermost breakline where the timber stops and the water depth drops off abruptly. If you catch a bass or two, then cast lures into the timber. If you don't catch any bass during your three trolling passes, there is probably nothing on that particular point; move down the shoreline to the next point.

cover-free breakline where the trees stop and the water depth sharply drops off. Once the three trolling passes are completed, put aside your trolling rod and fish the timber with flipping jigs, plastic worms, or jigging spoons.

Trolling a Sunken Gravel Reef
(Top View)

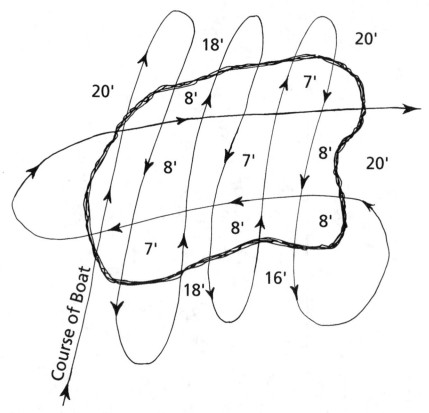

Cover-free mid-lake bottom structures can be thoroughly checked by trolling. To do this, simply make methodical passes back and forth.

29. On large, cover-free bottom structures that are relatively uni-form in depth, you can "snake-troll" the entire area by making repeated looping passes over it. An offshore reef comprised of gravel and small rocks is a common example.

30. When trolling in rivers, always troll upstream. If you troll down-stream, your boat will have to move faster than the current. This usually impairs your control of the lure's speed and depth.

31. One situation where you can troll in weedy water is when the weed growth does not come all the way up to the surface. If the

In effectively trolling a structure, you should be able to occasionally feel your lure bumping the bottom. If you don't, switch to a deeper running crankbait. Briefly changing the outboard's throttle speed may entice strikes from neutral or inactive bass.

water is 12 feet deep and the bottom has thick moss growing up five feet off the bottom, for example, bass may be holding randomly in holes in the moss, watching for baitfish swimming overhead. In this case, it would be wise to select a lure that only runs about six feet deep, so that it barely skims over the tops of the weeds.

32. Many trollers like to carry floating marker buoys. When a bass is hooked, they immediately throw a buoy overboard. After the fish is boated, they then put aside their trolling gear and cast a variety of other lures—keeping in mind that the bass was hooked 25 to 40 yards behind the buoy's location. Sometimes, if there are many bass on a structure, one may indeed have taken a trolled crankbait, but the others may prefer a jig, plastic worm, or other lure.

Index